T0278385

HISTORIC LOUISVILLE MURDERS

HISTORIC LOUISVILLE MURDERS

KEVEN MCQUEEN

THE
History
PRESS

Published by The History Press
Charleston, SC
www.historypress.com

Copyright © 2024 by Keven McQueen
All rights reserved

All cover images are courtesy of the *Louisville Courier-Journal*.

First published 2024

Manufactured in the United States

ISBN 9781467155427

Library of Congress Control Number: 2023946756

Notice: The information in this book is true and complete to the best of our knowledge. It is offered without guarantee on the part of the author or The History Press. The author and The History Press disclaim all liability in connection with the use of this book.

All rights reserved. No part of this book may be reproduced or transmitted in any form whatsoever without prior written permission from the publisher except in the case of brief quotations embodied in critical articles and reviews.

Dedicated to the one I love.

CONTENTS

Contents

ACKNOWLEDGEMENTS

Muchas gracias: Zoe Ames; Danielle DiGiacomo and the Carpenter Museum, Rehoboth, Massachusetts; Antiquarian Society; Eastern Kentucky University Department of English; Eastern Kentucky University Interlibrary Loan Department; Denise and Amber Hughes; Amy Hawkins McQueen and Quentin Hawkins; Darrell and Swecia McQueen; Darren, Alison, Elizabeth Renee and Charles David McQueen; Kyle McQueen; Michael, Lori and Blaine McQueen and Evan Holbrook; Chad Rhoad and everyone at Arcadia Publishing/The History Press; Craig and Debbie Smith; and Mia Temple.

Reader, I hope you are doing just fine. Friend me on Facebook and get news at KevenMcQueenStories.com.

Chapter 1

HOW McLAUGHLIN BIT OFF A NOSE AND CHEATED THE HANGMAN

There was a fire on Sixth Street, between Main and Water, Louisville, on April 18, 1842, that took the lives of a drunkard and a spaniel. A nearby neighbor, an elderly man named Patton, hastily removed furniture from his house and moved it into the alley, out of fear that the conflagration might spread to his home. After the blaze was extinguished, he was moving his items back inside when he encountered James McLaughlin, a Water Street tough who ran a "coffeehouse." In the parlance of the time, this wasn't the 1840s equivalent of Starbucks, but rather a place that served alcohol on the sly. The violence these establishments attracted was the stuff of legend, as we shall see more than once. McLaughlin walked up and stabbed Patton in the side, hand and chest with a bowie knife and then made himself scarce.

Patton, with the knife still embedded in his chest, walked to his house and sat down on the front stoop. He pulled out the bowie and cried to horrified bystanders, "I'm dying! James McLaughlin did it!" Then his soul was released from the thralldom of the body.

The dying man had identified his killer before an interested crowd, the knife was positively identified as McLaughlin's property and the wanted man was known to have a grudge against poor Patton. McLaughlin, you see, was about to go on trial for mayhem for having bitten off the nose of an unlucky fellow named Mike Cotter in a fight, and Patton was the chief witness against him. The arrest of McLaughlin was, in legal terms, a no-brainer.

McLaughlin's attorneys requested and got a change of venue. For reasons that don't appear in the record,, it took nearly a year for him to go on trial at the end of March 1843, in Shelbyville. The jury was undecided for several days but at last reached a guilty verdict on March 29. They had been hung, figuratively, but they determined that McLaughlin should be hanged, literally, for his brutal murder. The date was set for April 28, giving McLaughlin a day short of a month to live.

The Shelbyville jailer, Travis Wilson, received a constant stream of letters from busybodies instructing him how to do his job. He was irritated—and with good cause. Today, the sender of a letter pays postage, but in 1843, the *receiver* paid it, and Wilson had to fork over cash from his own pocket for the unsolicited advice. In mid-April, Wilson sent a notice to the *Louisville Journal* asking that all unwanted mail cease: "I request them to attend to their own business, as I shall undoubtedly to mine."

But McLaughlin was destined never to hang. On the day of his scheduled execution, he cut his own throat. It took him several hours to die, and during the interim, he said he had been framed and regretted that he would not have a chance to give his planned gallows speech. Jail authorities surmised that his wife—who had feared her husband might kill her and their child someday—smuggled a razor to him (though female attendants searched her whenever she visited), but in fact, the prisoner had sneaked it in himself when first committed to his cell. Not only that, but McLaughlin had also secreted a pair of scissors, with which he'd intended to kill Louisville prosecutor Nathaniel Wolfe while he argued against a new trial in court. McLaughlin had risen three times in the courtroom with assassination in mind but was stopped only by his belief that the governor would surely pardon him and murdering a prosecutor in court *might* spoil everything. Considering that the prisoner carried concealed weapons into the courtroom and his cell, those crank letters may have had good advice for the jailer after all.

McLaughlin certainly was one tough hombre. At his autopsy, doctors marveled at the number of scars and healed wounds his corpse bore. He had eighteen on his chest, neck and arms and a dozen more on his back, hips and thighs, each of which bore mute testimony to one of many injuries that, by all rights, should have killed him long before.

Barely more than a week after McLaughlin's suicide, a book about his life and crime already had been published and was on sale in Louisville. There is an advertisement for it in the *Louisville Journal* of May 6, nestled among notices for beaver hats, Byron collars (so you could look like Lord Byron, your favorite poet), phrenological diagrams and Brandreth's

Vegetable Pills, recommended for treating everything from skin blotches to the common cold to cancer.

In January 1844, the Kentucky legislature debated whether the Shelbyville jailer should be paid for keeping watch over McLaughlin—there was some question as to whether he deserved it, the man in his charge having smuggled in a razor and scissors and committed suicide—and whether prosecutor Wolfe should likewise be compensated for the expenses he incurred when he traveled to Shelbyville and unknowingly risked his life. My guess is that the second proposal was met with hearty yeas and the first with a chorus of nays, or possibly worse.

Chapter 2

MIND OVER MATTER

Mr. Baker (whose first name, curiously, seems to appear in no press accounts) and James Peters whiled away their time in Natchez, Mississippi, by gambling and cultivating hatred for each other. One day in 1841, they got in a fight after Peters accused Baker of cheating. Baker stabbed Peters with such gusto that the latter was crippled for life, unable to walk. Peters was in despair at this turn of events and made several suicide attempts while in the hospital.

At the end of June 1844, Peters moved to Louisville, where by then Baker was living. The handicapped man spent a few days drinking and brooding in Exe's coffeehouse. (For more on these sarcastically nicknamed establishments, see the previous chapter, about James McLaughlin.) He sought out Baker's home near the corner of Market Street, pretended to be in a conciliatory mood and, amazingly, asked if he could be his attacker's roommate. Even more astonishingly, Baker agreed.

All was seemingly domestic harmony until July 17, when Peters returned to the coffeehouse and asked to stay the night there. On July 18, he rode to Baker's home in a carriage and requested that the driver call Baker out. When the unsuspecting roomie strolled to the carriage to inquire what the man whose life he ruined wanted, the latter responded by shooting Baker clean through the body. Well, "clean" might not be the proper word. Peters calmly waited for the police to arrive and told the arresting officers that he had spent the last few years nursing a grudge and living only for the day when he could avenge himself. That desire fulfilled, he declared himself ready to shake hands with the hangman.

Baker died at sunrise on the morning of July 19. Peters was examined in court and committed to stand trial. Despite the cold-bloodedness of his obviously premeditated murder, Peters was acquitted. Maybe the jury just felt sorry for him because he had been paralyzed by his victim.

But it turned out that James Peters was not handi*capped* so much as handi*capable*—of high mischief, that is! In a surprising twist, soon after his acquittal, he married his victim's widow. Mr. and Mrs. Peters moved to St. Louis, where they were arrested in December for receiving stolen goods. They stayed together until 1849, when he "married another woman," the press informs us, implying that he committed bigamy, the self-punishing crime.

Mrs. Peters divorced her mate, became Mrs. Smith and moved back to Louisville, where she ran a Green Street boardinghouse. (The papers mention she rented "apartments" there that Peters had frequented in the past, which seems to be a discreet way of telling worldly readers that her house actually was a bordello.)

A bizarre incident occurred on June 21, 1850. Peters showed up at his former wife's doorstep and demanded entrance. She refused. Peters could hardly walk in, so he mounted a horse—with the greatest difficulty, one imagines—and *rode* in. He cavorted around for a while, then cantered back outside and ventured straight to one of those coffeehouses, which he also entered on horseback. Officer Kirby found his prey ordering liquor. Having learned the hard way how effective a weapon a knife can be, Peters whipped one out and threatened the policeman, remarking that his own life was worthless but he intended to sell it dearly anyway. Reinforcements appeared, and the evening did not end well for Peters.

We hear no more of him until August 21, 1852. On that night, Peters (still living in Louisville) fired several pistol shots at the woman he was currently cohabiting with—evidently, neither of his wives. One bullet got her in the arm. She survived, but Peters, fancying he had mortally wounded her, shot himself in the abdomen. He died the next afternoon and left behind nine dollars in banknotes, a French five-franc piece, a half-dollar, a quarter and a piece of paper on which he scribbled a note before shooting himself. It explained oh so much, yet oh so little: "Gentlemen: This is premeditated. I have no wish to live longer. I want us both put in one coffin and buried together."

Chapter 3

ON THE DANGERS

OF POLITICAL HUMOR

The *Louisville Journal* of September 27, 1842, featured a mysterious, vague editorial:

> *We are probably expected to give the particulars of a most melancholy occurrence that took place last evening. We have promised, however, not to mention it in our paper at present. We made the promise in reply to such an appeal as it would have been unmanly to resist.*

Having whetted its readers' appetites for a first-rate scandal, possibly a bloody one, the paper dropped the other shoe next day. On the evening of September 26, editor Godfrey Pope had shot librarian Leonard Bliss through the forearm, armpit and shoulder blade, the bullet's track stopping at the spine. Bliss wasn't dead yet, but he was not long for this bleak world. The reason for the secrecy was that a woman related to one of the parties was in delicate health, and it was feared that there might be dire medical consequences if she read about the incident in the papers. But after the examining trial, there was no way to keep it secret any longer.

The complex genesis of the murder: a few days prior, there had been a political meeting of Locofocos (a pejorative nickname for the Democratic Party) at Washington Hall. One member, Henry Pope, got intoxicated and started bad-mouthing his own party. Word got out, much to the jollification of its rivals, the Whigs (precursors of the Republican Party). Some persons thought Pope's drunken speech was so rich that they wrote it down and passed it around. Leonard Bliss showed a copy to the anti-Democrat *Journal* editors and asked if they would publish it. "But," added Bliss anxiously, "Henry Pope is a close friend of mine. Do you think it would offend him?"

The *Journal* men thought Pope would not be upset to see his words in print, as he had taken pride in his smart little speech after he sobered up—plus Bliss's rendition omitted the *really* bad stuff Pope had said. Thus, the extemporaneous drunken oration appeared in the September 20 issue under the headline "Closing Scene of a Locofoco Meeting."

Leonard Bliss. *Courtesy Carpenter Museum, Rehoboth Antiquarian Society.*

Perhaps Henry Pope was not offended, but another Pope was: his cousin Godfrey, editor of the *Louisville Sun.* He sent *Journal* editor George Prentice a letter demanding to know who submitted that speech. Not wanting to get his friend in trouble in that duel-prone era, Prentice asked Bliss what course of action he should take. Bliss thought about it, then decided it could do no harm for Godfrey Pope to know his identity as long as Pope didn't denounce Bliss by name.

But as we have seen, Pope did far worse than merely give Bliss bad publicity. Once he knew the writer's identity, he hunted Bliss through the streets until he found his quarry. Prentice ran an editorial on September 28 lamenting that things had come to this tragic pass, praising Bliss and noting that soon the *Journal* would probably have to run his obituary yet ending with kind words for the assassin. "We feel no ill will toward Mr. Pope," said the paper gently, even gingerly, "and most certainly we have no wish to see him punished unless the cause of justice imperatively demands it." Perhaps Prentice struck a conciliatory note because he was afraid Pope might come after him next.

Pope was arrested and held on $10,000 bail, which was raised. He was set free, one hopes with a cooled temper.

Meanwhile, Bliss suffered in his bed at the Exchange Hotel. So many guests and well-wishers turned up that doctors asked them to go away, as the patient needed rest. He died on October 6, age thirty-one; had he survived, he may well have been paralyzed. His funeral was held in the hotel on October 7. Pope was rearrested, this time on a charge of murder.

Pope's surprisingly brief trial began on April 14, 1843. On the next evening, the jury retired and, after half an hour, returned a verdict of not guilty. How did they reach this decision in the face of what appeared to be a cold-blooded, unprovoked murder? Bliss had, in fact, been carrying a loaded gun that night for fear of meeting Pope, and witnesses said he appeared to be reaching for it just before Pope fired. So going by the standard of reasonable doubt, Pope *might* have fired in self-defense. But witnesses also noted that Pope approached his victim with a veneer of fake friendliness and reconciliation, not unlike the sociable tone Moe often adopts just before putting Larry's nose in a vise, thereby putting Bliss off his guard until it was too late.

Godfrey Pope became a captain in Company E, First Kentucky Regiment Infantry (also called the Louisville Legion). There are two different versions of his ultimate fate. One holds that he died on the way to the Mexican War in 1846. The other is that in 1846, he drowned on a homeward-bound schooner that sank with all hands. Whichever is true, Pope sleeps a long way from home.

Chapter 4

A THING OF BEAUTY IS A JOY FOREVER

Mr. Henry William Keats, coal boat man and dweller in an alley between Main and Market Streets and Jackson, had muttered darkly about killing his wife. Word became deed a month later, on June 24, 1850, when Keats tried to "correct" one of his children with the swing of an axe, as advised by the ghost of Delbert Grady in *The Shining*. He missed, but on the second try, he hit his wife in the head, slaying her instantly.

(Do you suppose he was related to John Keats, the British poet? After all, John's brother George did immigrate to Louisville, where he became a wealthy philanthropist, and one account states that Henry William Keats was born in England. It would be a diverse family tree that included an immortal versifier, a humanitarian and an axe murderer.)

Keats lammed it out of the city, with the police in hot pursuit. As of June 28, no trace of him had turned up, and Marshal McMichael opined that he had taken an intentional final bath in the river. In actuality, the escapee had been hiding on the bank of a nearby canal. He employed a Black man to get news about his children and return with the same. Instead, the hired man went to the police and told them the location of the most wanted fugitive in Louisville. They didn't believe him. Too bad, because on July 1, a man who lived on Salt River saw Keats, caught him, marched him off to jail and collected the fifty-dollar reward.

The killer was remanded to stand trial. But on September 25, seven prisoners, including Keats, escaped from the city jail. The advertisement for his arrest informs us that he was thirty-four, stoop-shouldered and auburn-haired. He was rearrested the next day.

Keats's trial began on October 17. The jury swiftly found a verdict of first-degree murder, and he was sentenced to dangle between earth and sky on December 20. Almost immediately, his well-wishers—including, we are told, "some of our most influential citizens"—got up a petition to send to Governor John Crittenden. He refused to consider a pardon but granted Keats a respite until January 25, 1851.

A stroke of the axe for Mrs. Keats, a stroke of luck for Mr. Keats: in January 1851, the governor pardoned him. It is unclear whether this was the great idea of outgoing Governor Crittenden or incoming Governor Powell. There was a string attached: Keats had to leave the United States of America and thus become some other nation's potential problem.

Keats was gone, but the legacy of how he atrociously murdered his wife and so easily got away with it must have been an inspiration to the local lowlifes and spouse abusers. In January 1853, a fellow named James Bryan was arrested for threatening his wife with lingering death. His exact words to her: "I'll act Keats on you!" He didn't mean that he was going to recite "Ode on a Grecian Urn."

Chapter 5

IT IS ALL FOR NOTHING

It was one of the most notorious and pointless murders in Louisville history, perhaps notorious because it *was* pointless. It all started at eight o'clock on the night of November 18, 1851, when William Howard, a storekeeper and auctioneer, entered the White Mansion—yet another liquor-selling "coffeehouse"—at the corner of Third and Market. The place already had a bloody reputation: in October 1842, Talbott Oldham killed William Benham in the establishment and fled to Cuba.

Howard sought the proprietor, a harmless fellow named Henry Driehaus. Howard yanked Driehaus's nose. Driehaus ordered Howard not to touch him again. Howard struck him; Driehaus hit back; and then Howard pulled out a clasp bowie knife, eviscerated Driehaus on the spot with a wound six inches long and over four inches deep and made a quick exit. No one ever figured out his motive except that he was intoxicated. Somehow, the injured man survived, at least for a while.

Officer Humble arrested Howard. On the way to the police station, Howard offered Humble a bribe if he would allow Howard to enter the jail by himself so he could avoid social stigma—you know, because he didn't want neighbors to see him being carted off to jail after disemboweling a fellow human being. More likely, he had in mind a quick escape. Humble was not fooled.

Driehaus died early in the morning of November 19. As Howard was examined in court, an immense throng gathered at the White Mansion to sympathize with Driehaus's paralyzed widow or maybe because they "had a desire to look at his body," as the *Courier* admitted with unsettling frankness.

The murderer had no conceivable defense or excuse, so the court ruled he must stand trial. Reporters were requested not to publish details about the testimony, as it might prejudice readers so greatly against Howard that a fair trial could not be had. He was remanded to jail on November 24 while crowds outside the courthouse shouted that phrase all nineteenth-century killers dreaded: "Hang him!" Many of these vengeful ones were Driehaus's fellow German immigrants. The rabble was so rowdy that the prisoner's attorney, James Guthrie, said he had never before seen such public feeling against a client.

Nevertheless, in December, Judge Bullock refused a request for a change of venue. But it made no difference to Howard: soon afterward, the state legislature passed an act requiring that anyone arraigned for a heinous crime, such as sticking a bowie knife in an unoffending man's belly, could have a change of venue on request, providing two witnesses swore that they could not get an impartial jury otherwise. An announcement was made in July 1852 that the trial would be held in La Grange, Oldham County.

This long-anticipated event began in mid-November. The prisoner's four-man defense team had, remember, asked for a change of venue. Having gotten what they wanted, they now argued that the proceedings were illegal, since Judge George W. Johnston, who was substituting for Judge Pryor, was not a resident of the district, logic which would seem to make unlawful many trials held outside of their original venue. Additionally, the defense team waited until four days into the trial to bring this up. Johnston answered with the legal equivalent of "Nice try, boys, now go play outside," and the proceedings continued.

Howard's attorney Guthrie told the jury how Driehaus's German friends had "poisoned the minds" of Louisville citizens and turned them against his client. That might have been an effective argument in Louisville, but it is hard to see the relevance of the point, since this jury was in La Grange.

A defense witness, Harry O'Neal, swore under oath that Driehaus started the fight and Howard stabbed him in self-defense. What O'Neal said was demonstrably untrue, and immediately after his testimony, he fled before two indictments for perjury could be served on him.

On November 20, a year after the crime, Howard was found guilty and sentenced to be hanged in La Grange on January 14, 1853. The judge asked the prisoner if there was anything he had to say in extenuation. The best Howard could come up with was yes, he did stab Driehaus to death, but he didn't *mean* to.

A couple of days before Howard's scheduled date with destiny, Governor Powell granted him a twenty-one-day respite—not a pardon, which Powell said was out of the question, but three extra weeks of life to prepare for his end. Howard sent the governor a grateful letter, explaining that those so-called coffeehouses were the cause of his downfall. Meanwhile, the inevitable petition to spare Howard's life was launched. It soon bore signatures from five thousand people who likely would not have wanted to be drinking partners with the man whose life they endeavored to save. The list included seven of the twelve jurors who had condemned him to death.

Twenty-one additional days of life wasn't good enough for Howard, appreciative though he might have been, nor did he seem to put much stock in the effectiveness of petitions. On January 29, 1853, he broke out of jail. Governor Powell, who probably regretted his generosity, authorized a $500 reward for his capture.

Howard's jailbreak is a little side drama all in itself. Conspiracy theorists thought officials had been paid to change his trial venue to Oldham County, which had a jail more easily escaped from than Louisville's. Oldham's jailer, Thomas Head, was in big trouble. Being illiterate, he had someone write a letter explaining the situation, which the *Louisville Courier* deemed "the most miserable attempt at exculpation we ever read." Head protested that a rock-tossing mob of fifty had broken into the jail—not to lynch their idol Howard but to set him free. In February, five persons, including Head the jailer, were arrested on suspicion of being accessories in helping Howard escape. Head paid his bail, thus avoiding the indignity of being imprisoned in the same jail from which his charge had fled. Three of the accused paid fines, the assistant jailer was acquitted after a trial in June 1853, and Head was finally acquitted in September 1854.

But to return to the newly freed Mr. Howard: a groundless report held that he had been captured in Newport three days after his escape. On February 3, 1853, bystanders in Louisville saw a heavily bound man in a cart, guarded by twenty men, heading for the city jail. A large and curious crowd followed the conveyance in the rain. Rumor held that the man was Howard, but it was a suicidal lunatic named Rogers. On February 7 came a false story that the fugitive had been caught in Troy, New York; ditto a report of his capture in Maysville, Kentucky, in April. In June came a convincing report that Howard had been arrested in Florence, Alabama. The prisoner even had a glass eye, like the missing man. Not him. As late as January 1857, rumor held that Howard was a businessman in San Francisco.

The simple truth was that William Howard had cheated the hangman. But there is justice, and then there is Justice. The few legitimate reports of Howard's later life agree that he was a miserable wretch. He was heard from at the Cape of Good Hope in 1853. Then he went to Australia and appears to have ended up in California. A retrospective article from December 1870 mentioning the murder said that Howard "still wanders an outcast, the mark of Cain upon his brow."

Chapter 6

CAUTION: ELECTRICITY

In my 2012 book *Louisville Murder and Mayhem*, I made a passing reference to the hanging of slave Dave Caution, assuming that he had been executed for murder. This was a mistake, as he was hanged for attempted rape. But although it isn't a murder case, the story features points of interest, including the swiftness of the legal system in those days, the financial ramifications of hanging a slave and the grotesque thing that happened to Caution's body after death.

Caution lived in Bullitt County and committed his offense in Louisville on December 2, 1860. A German woman, unnamed in early press accounts but said to live with a minister's family, was leaving the post office when Caution approached. She asked for directions to the workhouse road. Caution and his White female companion (also never identified) said they would lead her there. Instead, Caution pushed her into the house of Charley Myers, a free Black man, and tried to have his way with her. After a fruitless attempt, Caution dragged her into the stable behind the house and tried again. She resisted until Caution finally gave up and left.

Caution was arrested on December 3; by January 21, 1861, he had been convicted and sentenced to be hanged on January 25. One might think, with good cause, that the very speedy trial and the death sentence for attempted rape were solely due to the defendant's race and status as a slave. However, having read hundreds of contemporary accounts of trials and executions, I can assure the reader that swift trials were the norm for both White and Black criminals and that sexual assault was considered a capital crime in those days. Not that being a slave helped his case any.

Any hopes for last-minute leniency Caution might have entertained were quashed on January 22, when Sheriff Wash Davis bought a rope. It was not for a clothesline. Caution, who had spent the past three weeks in near-continuous prayer, no doubt redoubled his petitioning to the Almighty.

Had Caution been just an ordinary lowlife, no one would have given a second thought to his worth. But he was a slave, which meant that he had a certain monetary value and that the state would have to recompense his owner. A panel that specialized in these things estimated Caution was worth $800 (translated into modern currency, $18,600). His owner (also unnamed by the press), although wealthy, was so stingy that he refused to buy Caution a pair of socks despite that $800 he was about to receive. Caution warmed his feet with a pair of stockings purchased by the jailor, Mr. Thomas.

Caution began his last day bright and early, spending the time praying. He told Mr. Thomas that he was certain he was heaven-bound and urged the kindly jailor to meet him there. At ten thirty, Caution was loaded in a furniture cart and taken to the corner at the intersection of Broadway and Underhill. There the gallows awaited him, not to mention about twelve thousand men, women and children. He mounted the steps bravely, removed his hat, admitted his crime and exhorted the crowd on matters of the spirit. He added pointedly, "When your time comes to meet God, I hope you are as eager to see Him as you are to see me hung." The trap was sprung at 11:20 a.m., and Caution fell three feet, but he was too heavy for the rope. It snapped, pitching him to the ground. He bravely remounted the gallows steps as officials made repairs. The second time, the drop was too short, and Caution strangled to death.

Then things got weird. Once Caution's death was ascertained, the body was cut down and carried to the Louisville School of Medicine at the corner of Fifth and Green. Before an audience of medical students, Professors Wright and Bayless applied an electric battery to Caution to see if he could be revived. (No one seemed to ask what they would have done if he *had* come back to life.) Legend claims the corpse sat up on the dissecting table, perhaps as students headed for the windows, but contemporary papers do not confirm the story. Again, lest anyone think this indignity was inflicted on Caution simply because of his race and status, performing electrical experiments on the hanged, like in *Frankenstein*, was fairly common at the time; I have collected stories of several incidents, both genuine and rumored. It must have just been considered the thing to do.

The School of Medicine added Caution's body to its stock of cadavers. Perhaps he expiated his crime by adding to the medical knowledge of surgeons in training. And whatever became of his victim? Evidently, the experience unhinged her mind. Soon afterward, she commenced leading "a dissolute life," as her obituary phrased it. She suffered from pneumonia and spent time in the city workhouse. She died in the city hospital on July 16, 1871.

Chapter 7

A BUNCH OF BENJAMINS

Louisville's Galt House hotel was the scene of several murders over the years, the most celebrated of which was when Union general Jefferson C. Davis killed fellow officer General William "Bull" Nelson in September 1862. But this is the story of a homicide that occurred on the premises several years before.

It was the autumn of 1854, and many strangers were in the city for the horse races. On the evening of October 2, Benjamin H. Lawrence of Louisville, called "one of the most successful turfmen in Kentucky," was in the hotel's entrance room. He had been keeping his spirits up by chugging spirits down. Alcohol makes everything seem like a good idea, and Lawrence was getting his jollies by pointing a loaded revolver at various patrons. He told a Mr. Ogden and William Glover that he would kill them if they didn't join him in a drink. They bravely, but no doubt diplomatically, refused his hospitality.

At last, he trained his gun on Benjamin Johnson, a horseman from Lexington, who did not share Lawrence's sparkling sense of humor. Benjamin no. 2 pulled out his own gun and aimed it at Benjamin no. 1. The peril of the moment sobered Lawrence enough that he tried to run away. Johnston fired four times in the hotel's rotunda. Two bullets entered a wall, and the others hit Lawrence in the shoulder and leg. (Or maybe it was the shoulder and hip. Accounts differ, probably due to the excitement of the event, and newspapers often got early details wrong in their incessant and sometimes underhanded efforts to scoop each other.)

B.T. Gividen. *Louisville Courier-Journal*, March 3, 1888. *Courtesy of the* Courier-Journal.

"[Lawrence's] wounds are not considered dangerous," said the earliest newspaper report. But then it *was* 1854, when some doctors thought moustaches prevented tuberculosis by filtering cold air, others theorized that washing the hair could ward off disease and others still practiced seemingly medieval remedies such as cupping, leeching and bleeding. Also, niceties such as antiseptics and sterilization of surgical instruments were years into the future. Perhaps it should come as no surprise that Lawrence died on the morning of October 6.

Although it was true that Lawrence had been doing something potentially deadly just before he was wounded, the fact that Johnson pursued and shot him while he was running away didn't look good. "Now that the man is dead, what course will the law pursue?" asked the *Courier*. Certainly, the death raised moral and ethical questions: Is it quite sporting to shoot a drunk, even if that drunk is armed and acting foolishly? What if said drunk is trying to get away?

On October 8, the court ruled that Johnson would be tried for manslaughter rather than first-degree murder unless the grand jury altered the charge later. Nevertheless, a murder-worthy bail of $5,000 was set, despite the prisoner's attorney's vehement protests. Johnson didn't happen to have that much handy, so off to jail he went.

The trial started in mid-July 1855. By July 18, the jury was hopelessly deadlocked. Four members wanted to convict Johnson for murder, seven were for manslaughter and one wanted to acquit. The jurors were dismissed, and Johnson had to be tried again. The second time around, he was found guilty of murder.

Johnson served two years, then influential relatives had him pardoned on the condition that he leave the country. He joined a Mississippi company that was part of General William Walker's famously ill-considered invasion of Nicaragua. His regiment was sent to the Chontales Department (district), where they behaved so atrociously that the Natives arose and killed them to a man. Being hanged arguably might have been a better fate.

Speaking of fate: the son of Johnson's victim, Benjamin Lawrence Jr., came to a bad end similar to his father's. Not long after Lawrence's death, his widow married John Churchill, cofounder of the famous Churchill

Top: Benjamin Lawrence lies where he fell. *Louisville Courier-Journal*, March 3, 1888. *Courtesy of the* Courier-Journal.

Bottom: Scene of the struggle. *Louisville Courier-Journal*, March 3, 1888. *Courtesy of the* Courier-Journal.

Opposite: Detailed death scene. You can make your own diorama! *Louisville Courier-Journal*, March 3, 1888. Courtesy of the *Courier-Journal*.

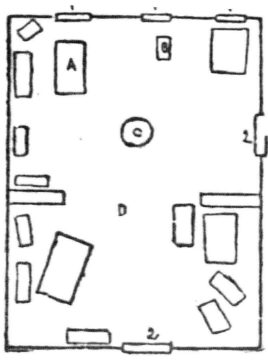

PLAN OF THE SCENE.
A—Desk.
B—Type-writer.
C—Stove.
D—Where the victim fell. Stock of furniture scattered promiscuously about the room.
1·1·1—Windows.
2·2—Doors.

Downs racetrack, home of the Kentucky Derby. Lawrence's three children were given an education at "the best schools in the country" and inherited $100,000 apiece when their mother died. None of these advantages helped Ben Jr. in the least. He frittered away his fortune in a few years betting on the races—horses are a recurring theme in this story, just as rats keep popping up in Stephen King's *1922*—and by the mid-1880s, he was a professional gambler and faro dealer. His assets were further reduced when Louisville cracked down on gambling. In 1887, he became co-owner of the Enterprise Vinegar Factory.

On March 2, 1888, thirty-three-year-old Benjamin no. 3 got drunk and entered John Shrader's furniture store in Louisville, where B.T. Gividen worked. Gividen owed Lawrence five bucks, and Lawrence wanted it *now*. He emphasized this point by striking his debtor with a heavy cane. The two men fought before two terrified secretaries, Leota Johnston and Nettie Newhill. During the struggle, Lawrence drew a gun. Gividen wrested it away from him and shot. Lawrence toppled over, hitting a "handsome oak bedstead" with his bloody head on the way down. He expired on the floor, surrounded by all the antique furniture that wasn't antique yet.

The next day's *Courier-Journal* included a sketch of the body lying on the floor and a detailed map showing the precise layout of the showroom/office that became his death chamber.

Chapter 8

HE'S A MANIAC, MANIAC

ON THE FLOOR

Forty-year-old Mr. Harrison of Boone County had a hopeless crush on Mary More, described as thirty-five, "fine looking" and intelligent. She lived with her father, Major John H. More. Harrison had been a widower for a year and sought a second helpmate; also, his heavily mortgaged land adjoined the More residence. Perhaps he thought a convenient marriage might be a way to get out of financial difficulty.

Harrison's late wife had been a More family niece, and they were married in More's house, so Harrison probably thought the family would welcome him with open arms. Yet he must have had some lingering doubts. Note that when he went to seek Mary's hand in marriage on October 3, 1876, he waited until the major was not at home.

Harrison popped the question. "No thanks," said Mary, or words to that effect, because she objected to his "dissipated habits," a then-current euphemism that generally meant he hit the bottle too frequently. Also, he had been acting a little weird lately. He let his house fall into squalor and told neighbors that he constantly had visions of his wife's tombstone. Everyone thought he was eccentric but harmless.

Harmless he wasn't. "No thanks" was not the response Harrison wanted. He shouted, "I'm crazy! I'm crazy!" and stabbed Mary More nine times in the chest and face with a jackknife. She escaped and locked herself in her handicapped brother William's room. By then, farmhands had been attracted by the commotion, and Harrison deemed it wise to hurry home and commit suicide. He aimed a rifle at his head, but it didn't fire. Time for

Not *this* William Henry Harrison.
Public domain.

plan B! Rather than sensibly leaping into the nearby Ohio River, he jumped into a cistern while bellowing his familiar refrain of "I'm crazy! I'm crazy!" It held only four feet of water, and he accomplished nothing worse than getting his clothes wet. His sons fished him out, and then Harrison made a beeline for the medicine chest seeking poison to gobble, but no such luck. He was captured and, the next morning, was sent to the jail at Burlington.

It was thought at first that Mary More might survive her multitude of wounds, but she succumbed a few days later. It was the sort of crime that has been committed many times throughout history, but the killer's full identity adds a level of interest. His name was William Henry Harrison.

"William Henry Harrison?" the historically astute reader is asking. "Was he related to the ninth president, who is chiefly famous for expiring from pneumonia only a month after taking the oath of office?" Affirmative! Harrison the murderer was the president's grandson. In fact, the More residence was located across the river from North Bend, a suburb of Cincinnati, Ohio, only fifteen miles from Old Tippecanoe's ornate tomb.

Some thought Harrison faked his insanity, but in mid-October, he was adjudged a lunatic and sent to the asylum at Anchorage, near Louisville. There we glimpse him attending the lunatics' ball in mid-November, just a month after his arrival. This monthly event was thought to calm the inmates; the *Courier-Journal*'s account bears the curious headline "Delighting the Demented." Among the eighty attendees performing waltzes, polkas and quadrilles were a "lithe and graceful" young woman who lost her reason after a cad seduced her; a man called Uncle Sam, because that's whom he resembled; an insane former preacher who hoarded rocks and buttons under the delusion that they were diamonds; George Maddox, an ex-Union soldier who called himself Sir William Gaylord whenever he didn't think he was General Sherman, though sometimes he believed he was a steamboat captain who died in an explosion; and George W. Scott, who thought he was killed nightly by poison and restored to life every morning.

Among these revelers was a man who went unnamed by the reporter but whose identity was unmistakable: "Another of the inmates, a spectator, was one whose ancestry [is] among the most distinguished in the country. A president of the United States was his grandfather. The fearful tragedy which took place in Boone County, some weeks ago, is remembered by many people here." Not sure if "here" refers to Anchorage or the asylum, but either is plausible; such was Harrison's brief and paltry fame.

Chapter 9

AND A MERRY CHRISTMAS

TO YOU, TOO!

John Mendel, about sixty and a respectable German immigrant, made his living as a woodcutter in Louisville. Naturally, he had the chief tool of his trade—an axe—lying around handy in his house. Someone else also found it very convenient.

After a certain disheartening event, it became necessary for John Mendel Jr. to tell police his whereabouts on the night of December 22, 1866. He explained that he had gone out on a date with his sweetie, Agnes Goodsell, and when he came home around midnight, he saw his father lying in bed with his head cloven like Old Nick's foot. The blood-soaked axe lay on the floor. The depth of the wound indicated that the attacker buried the entire axe-head in the elderly man's cranium, striking with such force that brain matter spattered a foot away. The younger Mendel sought help immediately, but his father died at nine o'clock in the morning on December 23, having never regained consciousness.

Mendel Jr. told the inquest jury that $768 was missing from his own trunk, so the obvious assumption was that the culprit was a burglar who didn't want to leave any witnesses. Two boarders in the same house, James and Ann Welch, testified that they heard no noise or struggling until Mendel Jr. woke them up. (The Welches were so badly spooked by the bloody murder that occurred in their boardinghouse that they moved out within three weeks.)

The inquest uncovered a discrepancy: none of the dead man's friends or neighbors had ever heard anything about Mendel Jr. having such riches. Frederick Leib, a friend of the elder Mendel, said that he understood the son had no money of his own. Mendel Jr. hastily explained that he wasn't in the habit of telling people about how much cash he had saved. In fact, he said, he had just loaned $500 to a friend named John Winan. He added that his father's money must have been stolen, too, as well as a missing book on witchcraft charms that he kept (for no home is complete without one).

Something about the seemingly earnest and grieving son provoked suspicion. Officer Hipwell noticed that Mendel Jr. had a bloody streak on the hem of his coat, which he tried to conceal by covering it with his hand. When Hipwell got a closer look, it was obvious that Mendel had tried to scrub off the stain. On New Years' Day 1867, Officer Sinkhorn searched the house and found the "missing" witchcraft book, which contained two promissory notes signed to Mendel Sr. totaling $1,250. John changed a key element of his story. The morning after the crime, he told Officer Henry Ryan that he had seen no one near the house when he arrived home except two policemen, but at the coroner's inquest, he transformed them into sinister-looking men whispering and carrying a bundle. Police located Mendel Jr. in a barroom and arrested him on suspicion of killing his father and staging the scene to make it seem a thief did it.

An examining trial was held on January 11. Much of the testimony was the same heard at the coroner's inquest, but some new, and very interesting, facts were uncovered. Junior desired to marry Agnes Goodsell, but Senior objected, and the two had quarreled. The deceased told a neighbor, Magdaline Endilen, about it. (Endilen also claimed she heard a man scream around midnight on the night of the murder, but she must have been mistaken on this point, since no residents actually inside the house heard it.)

Mendel Jr. had casually mentioned at the inquest that he recently loaned $500 to John Winan, but under oath at the trial, Winan declared he had never borrowed any money from Mendel, not so much as a shiny new nickel, let alone $500 all at once. Daniel Sauer testified that Mendel Jr.—rather than being flush with money, as he portrayed himself—had borrowed sums from Sauer often over the past two months.

Agnes Goodsell was asked what sort of coat Mendel wore when he visited her on the night of the murder. One made of black cloth, she replied. But when the police initially came calling shortly after the crime's discovery, he had on a brown velvet hunting coat.

The judge ruled that Mendel Jr. would have to stand trial for murder. The event came very soon, on February 6. But despite the preponderance of evidence against the defendant, the jury was deadlocked and dismissed. The case was rescheduled for the next term.

So it was that a second jury heard all the evidence over four days in the middle of May. After listening to twenty-two prosecution witnesses and an additional thirteen for the defense, plus taking a side trip to the house where the murder occurred, on May 22, the jury found Mendel Jr. innocent. Who knows? He might have been, but it seems unlikely.

What made such a favorable an impression on the jury? When his attorney General William Jackson asked, "You did not kill your father, John Mendel, did you?" the accused stood and answered with great feeling and sincerity, "As God is my judge, I did not." And that must have seemed sufficient.

Interestingly, over the course of the inquest and two trials, the *Journal* flatly accused Mendel in print of killing his father. In one big black headline, it called him "The Mendel Parricide." In another article, the editors referred to the legal proceedings as "this parricide case." And in the January 14, 1867 edition, a reporter stated: "We were perfectly satisfied on the morning of the inquest that the son was the murderer of the father; and the detective officers who allowed him to run the full length of the tether [and] allowed fact to accumulate upon fact until suspicion became certainty, deserve great credit for the skill with which they worked up the case."

Yet despite having been called the killer of his father, certain grounds for a whopper of a libel suit if untrue, Mendel never sued. Make of it what you will, if anything.

For a coda, let us fly forward in time to March 1890, when Mendel's defense attorney, William Jackson, in later life a judge, died of Bright's disease. On March 25, two days before the Great Tornado struck Louisville, the *Courier-Journal* published an overview of Jackson's earlier career by his colleague, Major Kinney, who bluntly recalled that Mendel "had killed his father with axe." He was not merely *accused*, mind—if we take Kinney's word, Mendel *did it*. Kinney noted that Mendel was still living in the city, though under an assumed name: "I recognized him as a recent prisoner in the city court for beating his wife." Perhaps she was Agnes from so many years ago.

Chapter 10

FIRST, DO NO HARM

Peddler Thomas Manly, a native of New York, and his driver Joshua Wood of Bowling Green, Kentucky, were plodding their way to Louisville in a wagon on February 12, 1868, and had got near Hays Spring, not far from the city, when a drunken highwayman on horseback appeared out of the brush. Most likely he said something witty and original, such as "Your money or your life!" Both travelers steadfastly refused to give him so much as a shiny new nickel.

Then the horseman did something strange. He neither threatened nor murdered but instead offered advice: "Don't go any further along this highway. There are men lying in wait who will kill you." He offered to protect the men if they rode with him. Manly and Wood accompanied the stranger a short distance, no doubt sensing a trap but feigning compliance. Then Wood lashed their horses and galloped at full speed toward Louisville with the highwayman in hot pursuit.

After a chase of a couple of miles, the man pulled up alongside the wagon and ordered the men to stop. They didn't. He drew a pistol and shot Manly in the jaw. After the attacker rode away, the travelers continued their journey. Manly remained conscious and conversed with his companion all the way to Louisville. They arrived at the city's United States Hotel at dusk.

Manly and Wood warmed themselves by the fire for a while. Manly stopped talking. Finally, the travelers retired. The wounded man died a couple minutes after lying down. An autopsy revealed that the bullet had ranged downward and cut his jugular vein. He must have bled internally for hours until weakness overshadowed his spirit.

When Mr. Wood described the killer to the police, they instantly recognized him as George F. Collins, an outlaw who lived in Mt. Washington in nearby Bullitt County. But Collins was no ordinary thug: he was also a doctor who evidently did not put much stock in his Hippocratic Oath. A plethora of Louisville officers traveled forty-two miles to Mt. Washington and found the doctor hiding in a back room of his house. He muttered to Captain John Martin, "I have got myself in a hell of a scrape, and liquor is the cause." The police brought him back to the Louisville. The whole round-trip affair took seven hours, which in those pre-automobile days was considered very speedy.

The prisoner was about thirty years old and the son of another Dr. Collins, a reputable and highly esteemed citizen, which seems to always be the way these things go. George Jr. had a wife and four children yet could not seem to stay out of trouble.

At the coroner's inquest, Mr. Wood testified that he and Manly weren't random victims. They had encountered Dr. Collins in the barroom of the Snapp House hotel, thirteen miles from Louisville on the Bardstown Road, a few hours before the fatal encounter. Undoubtedly, Collins noticed the traveling salesman's bankroll. Four witnesses actually saw the shooting from a distance, and all testified that after shooting Manly, Collins dismounted, stuck his finger down his victim's throat, then remounted and rode away. Perhaps the doctor considered his finger a diagnostic tool. But Wood testified that he did the same, hoping that if Manly vomited blood, he might recover.

The papers announced that Dr. Collins would be examined in Louisville City Court on February 14. The courthouse was packed with eager throngs that day, but they were disappointed when the trial was delayed. Perhaps they were satisfied by seeing George Sanders in court for stealing Zach Taylor's gloves, but probably not.

After a couple of delays, the doctor's trial began in early July. Collins's defense team admitted he was guilty but argued with straight faces that he was insane at the time. He had been drunk as a spider monkey when he shot Manly, so perhaps that was considered close enough. On July 2, the jury deliberated for an hour and a half, then found Collins not guilty, never mind the prisoner's guilty plea and what all those witnesses saw.

"The case is somewhat anomalous, and the result of the trial does not give general satisfaction." That was the *Journal*'s polite way of saying the verdict was unpopular. It became even more so as time went by. Having not learned his lesson, Dr. Collins got in several legal predicaments after his acquittal and even served time in jail. On January 28, 1870, he got in serious trouble again, this time at Mt. Washington. Characteristically, Collins was drunk and demanded that Perry Bishop hand over his watch. The farmer refused, so Collins shot him through the lungs. Then he forced Mrs. Bishop to hand over the timepiece, but at least he was all businesslike and wrote out a receipt for it.

The felonious physician escaped to Louisville, the scene of his earlier legal triumph. Two policemen found him on January 30, sitting drunk in front of the Sixth Street jail, of all places. He was arrested for attempted murder and for committing the 1870 equivalent of DUI (driving a buggy while inebriated). Collins downplayed the shooting and foreshadowed Monty Python by a century by hooting, "It was only a flesh wound!"

The result of Bishop's injury is masked in ambiguity. Contemporary newspapers do not confirm that Bishop died, so perhaps Collins was a better doctor than one might expect. Yet Bishop does not appear in the county's 1880 census, leading one to suspect he did die. On the other hand, an Oliver Perry Bishop passed away in Bullitt County on December 23, 1891. In any case, Dr. Collins was returned to Bullitt County to pay for his crime but released on bond. As predictably as night following day, he disappeared, leaving his trusting bondsmen in a pretty fix.

Chapter 11

JOSEPHINE LAWRENCE

MISSES THE TARGET

I t is amusing to see how the Louisville press jumped through hoops rather than state clearly how Josephine Lawrence, age about twenty-five, earned her lively livelihood. Women of her profession were called *nymphs du pave*, *filles de joie* and soiled doves. Josephine herself was termed a "cyprian," an "unfortunate woman" and a "lewd woman." At least reporters admitted she was "fine-looking." In plain English, she was a prostitute and successful enough to run her own "house of ill-fame" (again, the journalists' term) at 104 Lafayette Street. As events demonstrated, she certainly couldn't have made her living as a sharpshooter.

Prostitutes enjoy picnics just like everyone else, and on the night of May 18, 1870, Josephine attended one at Knapp's Garden on the outskirts of the city. She went without her boyfriend, Terry Ridge, who was infuriated by her temerity. In a drunken rage, he hunted her down and gave her a thrashing severe enough to knock out two teeth. Note that none of the picnickers tried to stop him. Afterward, the two returned to Louisville, leaving all those sandwich-eating witnesses agog.

Alone in her domicile, very drunk, very sore, likely very frightened and definitely very angry, Josephine Lawrence swore she would get back at Ridge. Around one o'clock in the morning, she took a loaded Colt Navy pistol that looked like a miniature cannon and staggered out into the big city looking for him. "I won't sleep until I kill him," said she, as determined as a nineteenth-century nymph du pave could be.

At the corner of Lafayette and Preston was the Spot Saloon. Josephine entered and saw Ridge drinking with buddies and likely boasting about how he'd just whipped his prostitute girlfriend.

Josephine aimed—she fired—she missed, hitting a bystander named Mike Lang from Peru, Indiana. Lang, whose now-obsolete profession was "hanger of ornamental fly paper"—fly paper that was prettier than the ordinary variety, I suppose—was carted off to a doctor. Police took Josephine to jail as she sobered up quickly and expressed great regret that she shot the wrong man. The record doesn't state what Ridge had to say. Probably something along the lines of "Whew."

Lawrence's unintended victim lingered two weeks and died on June 3, after suffering "the most intense agonies," the *Courier-Journal* tells us. He left a wife and three children. Ironically, Lang had been in town for only a week and had also attended the night picnic. He was on his way to his rented room when a friend offered him a drink at the Spot.

Now that she was officially a murderer, Josephine had to face an examining trial, on June 6. She was released on $2,500 bail. However, on July 12, she was "surrendered by her bail." That means whoever put up the bucks changed his or her mind and canceled it. Back to jail she went, but someone must have had faith in her. She got out again in mid-August on greatly reduced $1,000 bail.

On November 20, the press announced that Lawrence's case would be heard in court on November 28. But it wasn't. Or maybe it was. The existing copies of the *Courier-Journal* from that period are nearly unreadable in places, making the matter uncertain.

Then the case goes from uncertain to downright puzzling. We hear no more of Josephine's fate until January 1872, when the court said she would finally go on trial on January 12. As before, the date came and went with no action. Finally, and at last, she faced court on May 6 and was found not guilty two days later.

After the acquittal, Josephine Lawrence mysteriously drops out of Louisville history. It was customary, sort of, for prostitutes who got into trouble to change their names and move to another town, and that's probably just what she did. But we do know something of the further life of her violent mate, Terry Ridge. As early as September 1872, the *Courier-Journal* labeled him the city's "champion assaultist" when he was faced with a record five peace warrants in city court. Years later, he was tried on unspecified disorderly conduct charges, in May 1884, April 1888, January 1889, May 1890 and December 1897. His landlord took him to court in January 1886 for vacating the premises while owing $23.45 in rent. In June 1891, he was fined for driving an unlicensed wagon.

In October 1894, Ridge got in hot water for collecting thirty-five dollars from the city's firemen after lying that he needed the money to bury his daughter who died of scarlet fever. Swindling firemen seems to be about as low as humanity could stoop, but Ridge stooped lower. He did not mature with age and was arrested on January 22, 1896, for abusing his family, twenty-six years after he started a disastrous chain reaction by beating Josephine Lawrence. The news account sounds like something Dickens would have written and tossed in the waste basket:

> *Two years ago Ridge's wife died, and since then he has failed to provide for his children properly and has mistreated them on numerous occasions. The children were given food by the neighbors, but the father's actions finally became such that the case was reported to the Humane Society. When Agent Hild visited the place yesterday morning he found the sixteen-year-old daughter suffering from the effects of a severe beating, and the eleven-year-old son Will was just recovering from a drunken stupor, the father having allowed him to drink whiskey.*

In Ridge's last recorded offense, from March 1900, he was indicted by a grand jury for assault and battery against an unnamed person or persons.

Then there was the occasion in May 1896 when Ridge argued with butcher George Koch, merely because Ridge stole some lambs. When Koch dared retrieve his property, Ridge pulled a knife. Koch shot three times at his adversary and missed. Therefore, enraged people shot at Ridge at least twice and he escaped unscathed, an experience most of us will never have even once.

Chapter 12

MR. MILLER GOES TO GAMBLING HELL

What's past is prologue.
—*William Shakespeare,* The Tempest

Nineteenth-century journalists and reformers often called gambling dens "gambling hells," though the patrons of these establishments seemed to have a pretty good time. Benjamin Miller was an exception. But first, a little story from the past.

Louisvillian Joseph Croxton took an unexplained dislike to a man named John Hawthorn. On December 21, 1845, Croxton saw him asleep in one of those infamous so-called coffeehouses on the corner of Market and Floyd. Croxton hit his enemy upside the head with a brickbat, instantly breaking his neck. Then he stomped on the body and ran away. He need not have run, since the police were in no particular hurry to catch him. Allegedly, one officer said he *might* look for Croxton next week, if pursuit was convenient. The *Journal* ran an editorial on Christmas Day complaining about this lackadaisical attitude: "Here was one of the most open and brutal murders that ever disgraced a community, committed in the light of day, and yet our police officers hear of it and take no steps to bring the offender to justice…. If this is not giving scoundrels a license to murder whom they please, we do not know what is." The police must have been embarrassed by the article, since they assured the *Journal* men that they were taking secret steps to find Croxton. "We are glad to hear this," sniffed the paper, "though we greatly fear these secret efforts are not vigorous efforts."

The police eventually arrested Croxton, once they got around to it. He was tried and—amazingly, considering the indefensible circumstances of the murder—acquitted. Possibly he walked away from the experience thinking that he could not, or would not, be punished for such misdeeds.

Now we return to Mr. Benjamin Miller. Almost twenty-five years after Hawthorn's death, Miller and Croxton, both about fifty, were two of Louisville's leading "sports." They had long been close friends and, at one time, even co-owned their own faro bank (gambling saloon). On the evening of April 23, 1869, they got drunk at the Richmond Saloon on Market and Fifth Streets. After leaving, they argued. Croxton accused Miller of gambling using Croxton's money. Miller denied it. His so-called friend called him a liar. Miller swore at him. Croxton replied by punching Miller in the mouth.

After receiving the witty retort, Miller staggered off to Jacob Cassell's second-floor gaming saloon at 102 Fifth Street. But Croxton wasn't satisfied, even though he had "won" the argument, and slipped away to get a pistol.

The duo met again in Cassell's gambling hell. When Croxton entered, he saw Miller sitting at a desk and conversing with Cassell. Without warning, Croxton walked to within ten feet of Miller and shot him twice in the back, to the immense interest of other gamblers. Miller did not expire immediately. He sprang to his feet, grabbed his chair and pursued Croxton, who fired again and missed. The two grappled for the gun, and during the fight, Croxton hit Miller at least twice in the head with the gun. Weak from loss of blood, Miller seized a spittoon to toss at his assailant but sank to the floor and died thirty feet from where he had been shot. This time, Croxton was arrested and clapped in a cell without delay.

The preliminary trial began on April 29. The jury found probable cause that Croxton should be tried for murder, a whole new experience for him. This milestone occurred on July 8, after more than the usual difficulty in assembling a jury. At least 275 potential jurors were asked, "Have you formed or expressed an opinion as to guilt or innocence of the prisoner?" and were rejected by the defense team after honestly answering, "Yes." Of course, they might have responded affirmatively just to get out of jury duty, a civic obligation most people would far rather lose a toe than perform. Judge H.W. Bruce and attorneys from both sides complained that progress was impeded by the *Courier-Journal*'s previous articles on the case; they maintained that since everyone in town had already read details about the murder, it was too hard to find twelve unprejudiced men. Today, we call it "trial by media." The paper disagreed, because of course it would, but promised not to publish testimony until after the jury retired to deliberate.

Too bad for those jurors who were turned down, because while it lasted, the Croxton trial was the most gripping drama in town. And they would have had guaranteed seats in a courtroom packed with an estimated five hundred people—in sweltering summer weather. True to its word, the *Courier-Journal* didn't print any testimony until July 10, by which time there was enough information to fill two long columns of very small type. One of Croxton's defense lawyers was Judge W.F. Bullock—the same judge who had presided when the prisoner was acquitted of killing Hawthorn back in 1845. He and Croxton's other attorneys, T.L. Burnett, Isaac Caldwell and J. Hop Price, had their work cut out for them. To sum up: a drunken, belligerent man shot an unarmed foe in cold blood, and in the back, while the latter was unaware of imminent danger—and before a crowd of eyewitnesses, too. Not only that, but he had also murdered an unsuspecting, defenseless man once before. There was no way he could escape justice again, right? One wonders if local gamblers in their gambling hells wagered on the trial's outcome.

Before the jury, Bullock made a point of mentioning the overwhelmingly negative press his client had received before the trial. Cassell, proprietor of the gambling den, testified that just before Croxton showed up, Benjamin Miller had said, "Joe Croxton has been abusing me, and I can't stand it….It will all be over by morning." Bullock suggested that these words proved Miller had been athirst for revenge and threatening to kill Croxton and, therefore, the slaying could be considered self-defense. After all, they had engaged in an argument and a fight just twenty minutes before the shooting. Bullock noted that during this quarrel, Miller called Croxton a liar—and tossed in a profanity into the bargain. "Croxton is a chivalrous man, a Kentucky boy. Who would not feel insulted at such a term as that?" Furthermore, Bullock contended that Miller, with his pride wounded, had said to a Mr. Joe Shad: "I will have his life's blood before morning!"

Somehow, Bullock did not mention that his client had sneaked up on an unarmed Miller and shot him twice when his back was turned and he was chatting distractedly with Cassell. Nor did he acknowledge that Croxton had run off to get a gun and then sought Miller's whereabouts, which suggests premeditation.

Bullock also mentioned that a defense witness, a Major Rierson, was a "fine-looking man" and a Mexican War veteran who strongly resembled Kentucky politician John C. Breckinridge. What this nonsense had to do with establishing Croxton's innocence is hard to comprehend. The attorney also found a couple of witnesses who swore that Croxton's gunfire

John C. Breckinridge. If you are tried for murder, it pays if your witness resembles him. *Public domain.*

and Miller's chair-brandishing occurred roughly simultaneously, never mind what all those others present saw.

Bullock pulled a judicial rabbit out of a hat: he made a manifestly innocent man look guilty as an imp of Satan and a clearly guilty man seem innocent as a newborn fawn. It is only surprising that he didn't somehow find a way to blame everything on the spittoon Miller was clutching as he died.

The sole prosecutor, Colonel Phil Lee, made his closing argument on July 10, during which he suggested none too subtly that since Croxton could afford a three-man defense team, he was buying his way out of trouble. He also unnecessarily antagonized his opponent, Bullock, and complained about being constantly interrupted (which, in fact, he had been). He pointed out that after their initial argument, Miller did not arm himself; he merely went to a gambling saloon to cool off. The coroner found no weapons on his body. As for the piratical threat against Croxton that Miller allegedly spoke to Joe Shad ("I will have his life's blood before morning!"), Lee flatly accused Shad of perjury: "He is contradicted by every witness." The defense had claimed that since the bullet tracks in Miller's body ranged upward, he couldn't have been in a sitting position when shot. But a doctor testified that the bullets could have entered at that angle if Miller had been leaning forward.

Like the defense's Bullock, Lee for the prosecution had his rhetorical low points. He pointlessly ridiculed the last name of a defense witness named Banks, and just as Bullock irrelevantly brought up John C. Breckinridge, Lee invoked the shade of Benedict Arnold.

The jury retired on July 10 and announced a verdict of acquittal an hour and fifteen minutes later. The proclamation was greeted with hisses in the courtroom, perhaps from people unimpressed by witness Rierson's resemblance to John C. Breckinridge. "A mockery, I'll swear a mockery!" said someone. "A perfect farce!" shouted another. A reporter noted that despite the favorable verdict, Croxton "did not look like a happy man."

Although Colonel Lee lost the case, Louisvillians were so impressed with his closing speech that some requested it be reprinted in pamphlet form. In early October, printers Bell and Co. released a booklet containing a history of the trial and speeches by all participating attorneys. Reading it must have been considered the next best thing to being there.

One might suppose that after having been nearly imprisoned at best or hanged at worst, Joe Croxton would swear off gambling forever and go into a less risky profession, such as mucking out stables. But when Louisville outlawed gambling in March 1885—the same crackdown that so badly affected the life of Benjamin Lawrence Jr., as related in the chapter "A Bunch of Benjamins"—we find that by then, Croxton was running a gambling hell of his very own at 335 West Green Street. Interestingly, it catered to Black patrons. When informed that he was being shut down, Croxton was philosophical and magnanimous. "You bet we will close," said he, "and we ain't going to kick, either. We will go along with the balance of the boys [the other gamblers]. There is always bread for an industrious man." It is heartwarming to see that Croxton eventually learned to obey the law—and was even cheerful about it.

Chapter 13

"AND WIFE"

Twenty-seven-year-old railroad motorman Joseph Villier lived with his ten-month-old daughter, Lula, in a cheerless home at 1605 Seventh Street—cheerless because he was a widower. His wife, Lulie Kern Villier, died in 1897, ten months previously—the same age of the baby, suggesting that she died in childbirth.

Since that tragic event, Villier had been dating Nellie (or Neelie) McCubbin, twenty-three, a farmer's daughter who worked as a servant for Villier and his parents—dating her despite her bad reputation or, for all we know, because of it. The press explained that she "spent two years in the House of Refuge," a temporary home for the destitute—or, sometimes, drunkards and prostitutes.

At the end of August 1898, Villier's elderly mother kicked Nellie out of the house for undisclosed reasons, but the couple kept seeing each other. She was more serious than he about their relationship, whatever it was, and he refused to marry her. Or did his parents forbid it? Little did he realize that she had a jealous, vengeful, murderous streak. In addition, she was a meticulous planner, to the point of being obsessive-compulsive.

On September 14, Nellie asked Joseph to rent a hotel room for them. Perhaps he should have been suspicious when she asked him to bring the baby. He registered that night at the Enterprise Hotel at 234 East Market Street, signing the guest log "Joseph F. Villier." Nellie took the pen and added "and wife, Meadowlawn, Ky." after his name, as a handwriting comparison proved later. The notation may reveal what was secretly infuriating her.

Nellie McCubbin. *Louisville Courier-Journal*, September 16, 1898. *Courtesy of the* Courier-Journal.

In their room and away from prying eyes, Nellie—smartly dressed in a red shirtwaist, black skirt and sailor hat—gave a bottle of morphine-laced wine to Joseph and poisoned milk to Lula. Nellie herself did not partake. The baby expired quickly, but Nellie was dissatisfied with the slowness of Joseph's death. She had had the foresight to bring a revolver as a contingency plan and with it put Joseph out of his misery and then shot herself. She died holding Villier's hand. Not long before his murder, Joseph Villier told his family he had been considering killing himself and his child. Perhaps Nellie thought she would save him the trouble.

The next morning, porter John Taylor rapped on the door to alert the couple that breakfast was ready. When he received no response, he got that sinking feeling so familiar to hotel employees, due to hard experience, when guests don't answer their door. He alerted clerk C.C. Coots. At the door of room 4, Coots stood on Taylor's shoulders and looked through the transom. The newspaper illustration on page 53 reveals what he saw.

This tragedy has been played out by innumerable people innumerable times, but one circumstance was extraordinary. It appeared that Nellie McCubbin wrote a letter to her next of kin just before poisoning the drinks, and Villier spent his dying minutes doing the same. Hers read:

> *To whom it may concern: No doubt our friends will be surprised when they know all that I am going to tell. My sweetheart and I started out for a car*

ride. I begged him to take me and his baby and go to a room. It was my intention to drug him, for I love him and he loves me. His family and I could not agree. I have begged him to take me and leave his family, but he would not consent to do it. I loved him too dearly. He is now out to quiet the baby. Now is my chance to drug the wine. I went into a store at Fourth and Green and bought morphine, telling him that I got headache powders. He did not ask to see the medicine and, thank God, he did not question me. He had no thought of me killing him. I have drugged the baby's milk and I know it will die. I told him that I was going to write a letter to mother, and for him to take the baby while I wrote. I hope God will forgive me, but I did not want to live and do without him and his love. It almost breaks my heart to look at him and his dear little innocent baby. Just to think that within a few hours all of us will be lying here dead. I want to be buried with Joe. We came here as man and wife—Joseph Villier. I am going to pretend to him that I am going to take the letter out and mail it to mother, but of course it is a bluff. I want to be taken with him to his house and laid by his side in death. I want our graves to be side by side. This is my last request. I hope to God it will be granted. I know Joe will be pleased to know that I want to be buried with him. But he will never see this note. Now I will say farewell to all my friends forever.

None of the last wishes poor Nellie requested were granted. Villier's relatives refused to allow her body to be carried into their house. Neither are they resting side by side. He is buried in Saint Andrew Cemetery, while she is in Schardein Cemetery. His deathbed note read:

Oh! My God. Nellie has just told me that she had poisoned all of us, me, my baby and herself. Well, as I love Nellie my request is to be buried by her side in the city cemetery. I beg that never a mark be placed on our graves. Nellie and I wish to be buried Friday afternoon at 3 o'clock. Neither of us want a flower on our graves. Good-bye to all my friends. I did not know that Nellie had got the morphine. She told me that she got some headache powders. I would like for Will Roby, Frank Hinds, Charley Haas and Prack Jones to act as pallbearers for Nellie and I. Mother, bury me in a cheap coffin, and in the same clothes I have on. Don't do anything that I have requested you not to do. Mother, forgive me the trouble I have given you and father. I wish I could see you now. Would like to tell you lots but I can hardly sit up. So while I am awake, I will bid farewell to this world. I beg forgiveness for all deeds. Good-bye father, mother, sisters, and brother. Mother, tell Mr. Bess to see to my insurance and pay him for his trouble.

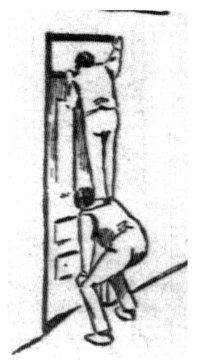

Left: Getting an unpleasant surprise when peeping through the transom. *Louisville Courier-Journal*, September 16, 1898. *Courtesy of the* Courier-Journal.

Below: What the transom peepers saw. *Louisville Courier-Journal*, September 16, 1898. *Courtesy of the* Courier-Journal.

Strange circumstances, but they got stranger. Villier's father, John, went to coroner McCullough's office, where he asked to compare the two notes. After a moment's scrutiny, he declared, "This is not my son's handwriting!" He pointed out that Joseph's penmanship was large and elaborate; Nellie's was small and crabbed. Both letters were written by the murderer, something neither the coroner nor the police had noticed. Additionally, comparing the notes leaves one with the distinct impression that both originated from the mind of a control freak. Despite what Nellie wrote in the forged note about drinking poison, an autopsy showed that only Villier and his daughter ingested morphine.

As Joseph Villier left the world, he did not realize what was happening to him. The victim's father remarked, "I could not understand why my son did not run from the room and save himself after he knew that he had been poisoned. Now I know it all."

Matters were clinched further on September 17. Coroner McCullough and John Villier opened a trunk left behind when Nellie was booted from the Villier premises, and inside was a third, never-mailed farewell note by Nellie, this one addressed to Joseph Villier's sister Susie: "I want to bid you farewell. Probably you will never see my face again. I want you to have my clothes. Don't tell your mother I wrote you this note."

It was dated three weeks before the double murder and suicide, proving Nellie had planned the crime at least that far in advance. If only someone had opened the trunk during the three-week interval, Nellie's evil plan may have been thwarted. Some people thought the note meant only that Nellie intended to leave the city in disgrace; others argued that if this were true, why did she leave her clothes to someone else? At any rate, people would have known she was up to *something*.

The *Courier-Journal* ran an editorial lamenting that no matter how often sordid crimes like this, which should serve as cautionary tales, took place, darned if people just didn't keep committing them despite the strictures of law, religion and common sense. But everyone thinks, "*My* case will be different!"

Joseph Villier. *Louisville Courier-Journal*, September 16, 1898. *Courtesy of the* Courier-Journal.

Chapter 14

WORKPLACE VIOLENCE

On a balmy day, May 29, 1872, two Black deckhands, William Reynolds and an unnamed opponent, got into a fight aboard the steamboat *Robert Burns*. A third Black employee, John Wagner, tried to separate them. Reynolds resented Wagner's intrusion and slashed him across the stomach with a penknife. The wound was a foot long and exposed the injured man's intestines. "The steamboatmen came to his relief," said a newspaper, "pushed back the entrails, dressed his wounds, and cared for him as best they could during the remainder of the voyage up the river." When they reached Louisville, they rushed Wagner to the United States Marine Hospital. The doctor said the victim bore the worst wound he had ever seen in his twenty-five-year medical career and prognosticated that he could hardly live two days.

Judge Price sent two policemen to the hospital to hear Wagner's side of it, but the doctor forbade their entrance, feeling it could only agitate his patient, who had a good pulse and was speaking coherently. The medic revised his original opinion somewhat. He believed Wagner might live several more days but could not fully recover.

When Reynolds faced the city court on May 30, an extra detail was revealed that the earliest accounts didn't include: Wagner had tried to stab Reynolds first. Reynolds was not released pending further investigation, but it looked like a case of justifiable homicide due to self-defense.

The doctor's prediction came true when Wagner died on June 19 after a very unpleasant month. In a historic moment, the first all-Black coroner's jury in Kentucky history met on the same day to rule on the death. They got to hear the dead man's voice, after a fashion—as you can, too, by reading Wagner's deathbed transcript:

> *Q: Have you any earthly hopes of living or recovering from your present wounds?*
> *A: No.*
> *Q: Do you think there is any possible chance for you to get well?*
> *A: No.*
> *Q: Have you given up all hope of getting well again? Have you made up your mind that you must die?*
> *A: All hopes are gone.*
> *Q: Who wounded you? Who hurt you and where did it occur?*
> *A: A young colored man by the name of Reynolds, I do not know whether James or William. He was grappling with another colored man as we were coming up the river thirty or forty miles below here. I endeavored to stop the quarrel.*
> *Q: Tell me how the whole thing happened.*
> *A: While Reynolds and another colored man were quarreling, I interfered to stop the quarrel when Reynolds and myself got to fighting when he drew a penknife, or rather a small knife, and hit me across the abdomen with a fatal wound from which I am now about gone.*

Three days later, the city's coroner Weber declared the inquest illegal. Perhaps he was upset at losing his fee. The *Courier-Journal* suggested as much: "[T]he coroner will be apt to make his point as well as his fee." He ordered a second inquest held at Wagner's grave in Western Cemetery, which means the poor fellow was exhumed and scrutinized again. The jury's verdict on June 24 had been predicted weeks before: Reynolds was acquitted.

The day before his acquittal, Reynolds got into another fight with another Black coworker aboard the *Morning Star* and cut his adversary with a cotton hook. This time around, offended sailors beat the stuffing out of Reynolds, and both he and his new enemy recuperated at the Marine Hospital—the same place where Wagner died a few days before.

Chapter 15

VALENTINE IS DONE

Afather died many years ago," began the article, "leaving a widowed mother and one only daughter with but little means to battle with the cruel world." It is worth noting, just to show what changes time wreaks, that they were considered to live way out in the sticks, though their five-room log house was merely four miles from Louisville, on a piece of land between the Manslick and Seventh Street Roads.

The daughter was Elizabeth "Lizzie" Wirtz, who, though living in disadvantaged poverty, was by young adulthood rich in two respects: she was good-looking, and she had two suitors.

One was Jacob Rein, age twenty-one, who had courted Lizzie for five months and been engaged to her for three. This was not at all to the liking of her other pursuer, Valentine Rabbitt, who claimed to be twenty-three, though scoffers said he was only seventeen. He had made Lizzie's acquaintance back in April, and though she did not encourage his advances in the least, he often dropped by the Wirtzes', ostensibly to visit her brothers. Sometimes he even showed up when Rein was there. The two rivals seemed friendly on the surface, but one suspects they gave each other the stink-eye when Lizzie wasn't looking. Later, Lizzie denied that Rabbitt had been sweet on her, but the denial may have been born of embarrassment.

No matter how hard Rabbitt tried, he could not break Rein's grip on Lizzie's heart. Jacob and Lizzie set a wedding date: Sunday, June 25, 1871. Valentine realized that if he was going to win her, drastic measures must be taken.

On the night of June 19, a week before the wedding date, *someone* shot at Jacob as he was entering the Wirtz residence and barely missed. Naturally, his opponent Rabbitt was suspected, but no one did anything about it.

On June 25, the bridegroom asked Lizzie if she would mind postponing the ceremony until July 2, since his job was about to end and he would soon have both money and time for a grand honeymoon. The couple strolled the yard, making plans for the years ahead. In the afternoon, along came that third wheel Valentine Rabbitt, all smiles and seeming benevolence. "Harmony and good feeling prevailed," said an early chronicler. "Not a word was spoken, nor was there a look which indicated anything but kind feelings and a generous rivalry." Lizzie and Jacob *did* notice a four-shooter pistol sticking out of Valentine's pocket, but hey, it was a rural area where nearly all men went armed.

Rabbitt made a good-natured pest of himself until ten o'clock at night, when he finally left the house. The happy bridegroom Rein departed fifteen minutes later and had scarcely walked a couple hundred yards when Valentine Rabbitt sprang up from a fence corner, pistol in hand. "I know you, Valentine," Jacob said. "You are not going to shoot me, are you?" Rabbitt fired at his stomach and ran away.

The house's occupants heard the shot. Lizzie asked her stepfather, Mr. Weis (or Weiss), to investigate. He demurred out of fear that he might also be shot. Lizzie replied, "If he be dead, I wish to die also. I will go to him if a hundred guns were pointed at me." She and her mother—but not Weis, who undoubtedly was mortified when the story hit the papers—ventured outside and found Jacob lying barely alive in a field. They carried him to the house and tended to him until the doctor arrived and said Rein could not survive.

Justices John Schardine (or Shardine) and S.A. Gaar reached the house in haste to take Rein's dying statement. "Who shot you?" they asked.

"Valentine Rabbitt. I knew him before he shot me, and when he shot me."

"Did you have any difficulty with him before the shooting?"

"No."

Coroner Conrad Weber arrived and asked, "Do you think that you will die?"

"Yes."

"Don't you think that you will get well?"

"No."

(The reader may have noticed that this strange line of questioning is very similar to the Q&A session held with the dying steamboat worker John Wagner in 1872, as recounted in the chapter "Workplace Violence." Why did the authorities ask such repetitive, yet slightly varying, questions?

Evidently, to ascertain whether the dying victim was "in his sound mind." If so, his words could be used as evidence in court.)

Lizzie tended to Rein right to the end. He wanted to will all his worldly belongings to her, but he died at 1:05 a.m., before the county attorney came. Lizzie kept her deepest feelings inside until his death, and then the floodgates opened. The coroner's postmortem proved that the bullet had lodged in Rein's spine and that he bled to death internally.

The next day, a constable arrested Rabbitt as he worked in a harvest field. He swore many an oath as he was led to jail, protesting that he and Rein were great pals. After invoking a curse from the Deity, he said, "Were we not together yesterday evening, and did I not appear and act friendly toward him?"

Rabbitt went on trial on December 6 and summarily was found guilty. The only question was the penalty. If Valentine had any skepticism that he would hang, that doubt was removed on December 21, when he was sentenced to go to the gallows on February 9, 1872. The defense offered seven arguments for why they felt Rabbitt had not received a fair trial, but Judge Bruce swatted each down in laborious, legalistic detail, citing many authorities and much precedent.

The only convincing pro-Rabbitt testimony came from Dr. Blackburn, who said the bullet he extracted from Rein's body was too large to have come from the gun Rabbitt was supposed to have carried. If true, this would have been fine exculpatory evidence—but since this point was not mentioned during Rabbitt's appeal, it must not have been as exonerative as his lawyers initially thought. A reporter noted at the time that Rabbitt "seems to have owned" a small Sharpe's pistol, and his phrase suggests that this important detail was not nailed down to a certainty. And it is a fact that Rabbitt was armed on the night of the murder, since Elizabeth and Jacob saw his gun.

The condemned man's attorneys appealed to a higher court, which guaranteed a delay in the execution. In May 1872, Rabbitt got a double dose of bad news: the appeals court affirmed the verdict, and the governor signed the death warrant. The new date was set for July 26. This was much to the disgust of the *Courier-Journal*'s Small Talk columnist, who was against the death penalty:

> *A public murder is announced to take place in Louisville in July. The people of this city ought not to permit such a thing if they can prevent it by protesting against it. Hanging a murderer can never bring back to life the*

murderer's victim, and a community like ours cannot afford to lose sight of the brutalizing effects of a gallows scene. There is a method of punishment which is simple, and which does not place the murderer in the position of a martyr and a hero.

The writer was referring to jail time, which, come to think of it, *also* cannot restore the life of a murder victim and often makes martyrs and heroes of prisoners.

Somehow, Rabbitt won an extra couple months of life, making his new scheduled final day September 27. The *Courier-Journal* ran a gloomy and dispiriting interview with him the day before:

Q. Do you feel that when your time comes to die you will be ready?

A. Yes.

Q. Have you any hope of escaping death?

A. I don't know of any chance. I only know that I am innocent and not afraid to die.

Q. Is it a consciousness of your innocence that strengthens you under the circumstances?

A. Yes.

Q. Do you believe in Christianity, in the future state of the soul, in future rewards and punishments according to your actions in life?

A. Yes.

Q. Then, with this belief, can you declare till the last that you are innocent of the murder?

A. Yes, all I can.

The reporter mentioned that Valentine's friends and family were agitating for a last-minute reprieve on the grounds that new evidence would cast doubt on his guilt. Later, it was revealed that a hasty letter from coroner Weber gave Governor Leslie reason for pause and the governor commuted Rabbitt's sentence to life in prison at Frankfort. The evidence would not be publicly released for a couple of years.

Rabbitt's life sentence, it turned out, was not very long at all. The young prisoner took ill and died of pneumonia on October 25, 1874. The *Courier-Journal* headlined the story "Gone to Another Judge." As for that new evidence that saved his neck, a reporter remarked: "We are in possession of these facts, but action in [Rabbitt's] behalf has not been made because the chain of evidence looking to his innocence has never been sufficiently complete." In other words, it was good enough to create hesitation but not good enough to get him out of the pen.

A month later, the paper finally revealed the evidence in an article titled "Was He Guilty?" The obvious purpose of the piece was to sow reasonable doubt about Rabbitt's conviction. Some bits of proposed evidence were more convincing than others, but none of them were world-beating. One argument was that because Rabbitt was unpopular and the community thought he was guilty, he received what we now call a "trial by media." Another was that the jailer described him as being "kind and obedient" in prison, which proved nothing. His actions on the night of June 25, 1871, were relevant, not his prison demeanor.

It was alleged that an extra set of shoeprints was found in the area near the murder site—but who could say definitively who made them, and when? Supposedly the prints didn't match Rabbitt's shoes but did match those of a man named Herman Ernst (or Earnst), which would hardly be surprising, since he lived only a few hundred yards away; in fact, Jacob Rein boarded with him. Also, Coroner Weber found these tracks while investigating the crime scene the day after the murder, so why did he say nothing about it at the time?

It will be remembered that someone took a potshot at Rein a week before his death and missed. The reporter said that Lizzie's stepfather, Mr. Weis, suggested to Rein that Rabbitt had fired the shot and thus Rein was in the frame of mind to blame Rabbitt when an assassin shot him. It only makes me wonder why Rein spent hours with Rabbitt that evening, and even seemed to have a good time with him, if Rein thought Rabbitt had recently tried to kill him.

There was fancy stuff in the "new evidence" about the moon shadows that night and how the killer could see Rein clearly but not vice versa; yet if Rein's version of events was true, he had a short conversation with Rabbitt just before the shooting and could have recognized his voice.

Then we must consider coroner Weber's letter of September 23, 1872, to Governor Leslie, the one that rescued Rabbitt from the waiting noose, the contents of which were only now revealed. Weber stated three "facts, which were not in evidence at either of [Rabbitt's] trials." He failed to explain why such important life-or-death truths had not been entered into evidence—twice! The first point Weber made was that on the day of the examining trial, Weis's neighbor Ernst asked Weber to be excused as a prosecution witness. After the coroner granted the request, Ernst left, and when he returned, he confided that he had found a double-barreled pistol at the murder scene with one barrel empty. When the coroner asked who owned the pistol, Ernst answered that it belonged to either himself or his son—Weber could not remember which, more than a year after the event. This suspicious weapon appears not to have provoked Weber's curiosity. The coroner assured the governor that he told the prosecuting attorney about it at the examining trial, but it is not mentioned in any accounts of the trial—as it certainly should have been, since it would have been a showstopper. What happened to this gun? Was it ever test fired to see if its bullets matched the one that killed Rein?

Later, the coroner wrote, he went to Ernst's house, where Rein had been a boarder. In Weber's presence, Ernst and Mr. Weis opened the unlocked trunk and found that Rein's money was gone. "Where did the money go?" Weis asked. "You have it," answered Ernst. The implication was that Ernst and Weis conspired to kill Rein for profit. Weber assured the governor that he had requested that Ernst testify concerning the pistol and the missing money, but Ernst didn't. And yet the coroner sat on this vital information for over a year, until it looked like Rabbitt was going to be hanged.

The coroner's final aspiring bombshell was that when he first arrived at Mr. Weis's house, Jacob Rein was comatose and had to be revived. "I had to arouse him to get him to answer my questions; some of his answers were given only by a nod of his head, and he died in less than thirty minutes after I arrived at his bed." But no one else at the scene appears to have agreed with this, and the earliest newspaper accounts depict Weber conversing clearly with the dying youth. Perhaps coroner Weber was perfectly honest in his letter to the governor. But he sounds rather like a man who is willing to tell "harmless" fibs if it will save some poor wretch from the gallows.

After unveiling the coroner's letter, the Rabbitt-supporting reporter said the chief evidence against the prisoner was Jacob Rein's dying declaration but added that people put too much stock in deathbed statements—and yet the reporter (and others) were convinced by Rabbitt's own final assertions that he was innocent. Indeed, this seemed to be the reporter's pièce de résistance. Rabbitt's last words before he died were, "I know nothing of the murder of Jacob Rein but now feel as though the guilty parties will soon be brought to justice." The reporter lamented, "The fact that he emphatically professed [his innocence] not only on the night before the day fixed for his execution (when he knew nothing of his reprieve), but that he did the same in his last illness when assured that there was no hope of recovery, ought to be entitled to great weight in modifying the harsh public opinion which he suffered in life." So Rein's dying statement didn't count, but Rabbitt's did?

Yes, it is theoretically possible that Rabbitt was innocent and someone else with no discernible motive shot Rein just a few minutes after Rabbitt left the house, putting aside that Rein knew Rabbitt and clearly identified him as the killer. But "possible" isn't synonymous with "probable."

What of Lizzie Wirtz, who bravely came to the aid of her mortally wounded fiancé? Marriage records show that an Elizabeth Wirtz married Frederick Klotter in Louisville on December 2, 1872, a year and a half after the murder. It looks like she renewed her life after the tragedy.

Chapter 16

COFFEE, EXTRA BITTER

Louisville's criminal element was busy in the summer of 1857. The *Courier*'s police blotter column for July 29 tells us J.A. Williams, a deaf-mute loafer, was arrested for public intoxication and disorderly conduct. "He is unfortunate, but that's no excuse for drunkenness," argued the author. Caroline Matthews, a crazy woman with "one eye in deep mourning" (meaning she had a black eye) was held for getting drunk, breaking things and stealing a Dutchman's clothes. Catharine Smith got drunk and beat her husband; she was so wild the police had to haul her to jail in a furniture cart.

Amid this action, stonemason John A. Comstock and his wife, Sophia, were key players in a mystery enacted in their home on the corner of Washington and Hancock Streets. On Tuesday, July 28, they went out to visit. When they came home, they drank coffee and had been ill ever since, Sophia violently, John much less so. It was theorized that a villain sneaked into the house while they gone and poisoned the coffee. Mrs. Comstock's world ended on July 29. Her husband recovered quickly. The couple had been married only eight months.

"The testimony in the case before the coroner's jury was altogether circumstantial, and as the awful deed will be legally investigated, we forbear giving particulars," said the *Courier*. Perhaps the paper was concerned with protecting the privacy of the accused before a trial. On the other hand, it sounds like the jury was privy to information of such nature that the paper feared a libel suit if it published details. Despite the *Courier*'s seeming reticence, it gave away the big secret in the same issue.

The Comstocks lived alone but, at the time, were hosting Sophia's fifteen-year-old niece with a lovely name, Alice Ion Ransom, usually called Ion. Ion lived a life that sounded like a Dickens novel. She worked to support her insane mother, and her father, a well-known Louisville painter, had committed suicide in a bizarre manner about five years before. A reporter reminisced that he "drowned himself in the river at the foot of Fifth Street.… He had walked into the river and was found drowned, standing erect in the water, his face under the surface, and his shoulders just visible."

Ion had not drunk the coffee. The jury's verdict was that Mr. Comstock likely poisoned the breakfast beverage with assistance from his niece. This theory required one to believe that John Comstock drank just enough arsenic to make himself ill but not enough to kill, to fool investigators into believing a stranger did it. It was possible but would have required spectacular bravery and foolhardiness. Ion was not in the house while her aunt and uncle drank the tainted coffee but rather was working at her job at Weinhoff's upholstery shop.

The pair were hauled before court and arraigned on July 31. A reporter said, "The man is a tall, rather rough looking, middle aged man, while the other party is a pale young girl, who was much distressed at her position, protesting that she knew nothing whatsoever of the fatal affair."

Detailed testimony was taken on August 2. Dr. Charles Metcalf testified that Mr. Comstock had come to his office on Tuesday the twenty-eighth and asked him to treat his sick wife. Observe that Comstock felt spruce enough to go outside and seek a doctor. During the house call, Metcalf found the woman vomiting and saying she had been sick since breakfast. She opined that she had been poisoned. Metcalf noticed two coffee cups on the table, one empty and one nearly full. He must have had suspicions even then, since he tested the coffeepot, but he found nothing unusual. Mr. Comstock said he felt sick too, so the physician gave medicine to both. But he noticed that Comstock seemed fine. Even his pulse was normal.

Dr. Knapp visited the same morning. He said that he thought both patients had been poisoned. Mrs. Comstock was clearly much sicker than her husband; Knapp agreed with his colleague that Mr. Comstock had a natural pulse.

Hugh Hayes testified that he dropped in to see the Comstocks on the deadly morning and the husband had confided that he thought Ion poisoned their water: "He said his wife had reprimanded the girl for the company she kept and had no doubt she had poisoned them for revenge." Ion had applied ice to Comstock's head, and as she left, Comstock told Hayes, "See, she knows all about it."

Dr. Bayless, who performed the postmortem, said Sophia's stomach bore evidence of irritant poison yet was not much inflamed. On the other hand, if she had received a large enough portion of arsenic to kill her quickly, her stomach might not be much swollen.

Professor Smith had examined the breakfast articles and testified that there was no poison in the sugar but twenty grains of arsenic in one pint of coffee from the coffeepot, and a single grain could cause death. Here was a troubling mystery: how come Dr. Metcalf found no arsenic in the coffeepot but Smith did? Smith added that only one sip of that pestilential coffee should have killed Mr. Comstock. Surviving would have been "a miracle." But Comstock said he drank an entire cup and took two sips of another.

Adam Smith, clerk at Owen's drugstore, said Ion Ransom wanted to buy ratsbane there on Saturday, July 25. "I don't like to sell it," he hesitated. "There's no danger. We have rats," she replied. Smith sold her half an ounce.

John Bottom testified that Ion did something exceedingly weird in the graveyard the next day, July 26. She reached into her pocket and pulled out a packet labeled "poison." Bottom was alarmed and performed a strange action himself. He ripped the "poison" label off the packet and tore it to shreds. "Oh, it's just to poison rats. You shouldn't have torn that up," Ion said. It appears that no one in court asked Bottom to explain why he did that. Three days later, Sophia Comstock was dead—but from arsenic, not ratsbane.

Mary and Angeline Bottom told a story that was the reverse of the one Mr. Comstock told Hugh Hayes: Ion told them Comstock, not his wife, was the one who had objected to her visiting "a certain girl."

After these proceedings, Comstock went to jail and Ion was released on bail, which her attorney paid.

The examination continued on August 4. John Wolverton related how he had gone to the upholsterer where Ion worked to urge her to see her dying Aunt Sophia. Ion seemed "terribly shocked" by the news. When they got there, Wolverton thought John Comstock appeared to be doing well, all things considered.

William Ray had dropped by the residence after Sophia died. "Do you suspect anyone of doing this?" Wray asked Comstock, who replied that he didn't. Then John and Ion left the house together and seemed friendly, which surprised Ray, because he had heard of Comstock's accusation against her.

Ion's aunt Mrs. Wolverton testified that she had seen her sister Sophia before she died, and that Sophia said, "I am suffering for an innocent person, dying for another woman." But she passed away before she could explain this extraordinary statement. In addition, she told Mrs. Wolverton that she didn't think John drank any coffee, no matter what he said. The witness had seen Mr. Comstock ransacking his wife's deathbed looking for something, saying he was searching for money to purchase medicine, though he had cash in his pocket.

All of this was prosecution testimony. The defense offered none whatsoever. The defendants' attorneys pled on their behalf. Comstock's lawyer Ormsby said his client was a poor laborer who loved his wife. Ion's advocate, L.H. Rousseau, blamed Uncle John Comstock, whom he painted as "a man of previous bad character and worse associations." Ion "was guileless and unpracticed in the ways of the world." There was no evidence against her, said Rousseau, except for the coincidence that she happened to have ratsbane in her possession.

On October 14, the grand jury returned true bills against Comstock and Ransom, which means the jurors felt the evidence against them was sufficient to proceed with murder trials. Comstock's would be first, and it began that very day. He was found not guilty on October 15. He thanked the jury and said, "I must once more see the grave of my poor wife." But he was right back in jail on January 20, 1858. He had tried to leave the state without paying his lawyer's fee.

Ion had her day in court in May 1858. Since the alleged mastermind behind the crime was acquitted, it seemed a foregone conclusion that the supposed accomplice would be, too—especially since she was female and a teenager and had a tragic family background. I found no proof she was acquitted, but clearly she was, since the *Courier*'s marriage licenses column on November 26, 1859, informs us she had just married John Seller. Let's hope her lot in life improved.

In retrospect, there are plenty of contradictions and circumstances that make the Comstock poisoning case puzzling. It is suspicious that when the doctors visited, Comstock pretended to be sicker than he was, and there is no doubt that Ion bought poison a few days before Sophia's death, but it was the wrong kind. On the other side of the ledger, how come one expert found poison in the coffeepot while another didn't? Some witnesses said Comstock tried to cast blame on his niece Ion, but if they were partners in crime, why draw suspicion to her? For that matter, if either John Comstock or Ion Ransom were guilty, why didn't they ditch the poisoned coffee before the doctors and police showed up?

Chapter 17

HOW TOM SMITH BROUGHT UNWARRANTED DISREPUTE UPON THE CROTON OIL INDUSTRY

Mrs. Joseph Breeden (or Braden) visited a neighbor on the evening of May 18, 1871, then returned to the grocery store/residence where she lived with her husband on the Salt River Road, twelve miles below the city. She found Mr. Breeden dead behind the counter with a bullet wound in the head. The murder had occurred within the past few minutes, so she barely missed being killed herself.

Within a few days, the police had an excellent suspect: habitual thief Thomas Smith, a Black Louisville resident arrested for carrying a concealed weapon. Several witnesses, Black and White, saw him at Breeden's store on the evening of the shooting. The killer stole two pistols from the store, one of which was found on Smith. A witness named Thomas Sherin described the gun and its belt perfectly without seeing it. There was enough evidence to convict Smith in the spring of 1872. His hanging was scheduled for October, but the penalty was delayed when his lawyers appealed to a higher court.

It appeared that Smith might meet his Maker by natural means. In September 1872, there was a smallpox outbreak at the Louisville jail, where he was held. This was a highly contagious, usually fatal, nearly always disfiguring illness that sent our ancestors into paroxysms of panic that made the modern reaction to COVID-19 look like cotton candy and circus peanuts in comparison. Yes, people in Smith's time sure were scared of smallpox!

Studio audience: *How scared were they?*

They were so frightened that communities panicked at the slightest rumor that the disease was afoot. In April 1861, a Philadelphia doctor triggered a mass panic when he stepped aboard a crowded horse-drawn train car and remarked, "Smallpox is in this car—I can smell it." The car was empty within moments, which may have been his object if he wanted a seat.

When Rome, Indiana, had an outbreak at the end of January 1864, farmers wounded themselves in the pocketbooks by refusing to sell food in town.

The body of a Washington, D.C. man who died of smallpox in January 1846 rotted so badly that it almost fell to pieces in its coffin. The next month, a Philadelphia man whose head turned black from the disease went insane and tried to leap from a window. An interested crowd of spectators kept a respectful distance lest they catch it too.

A couple of Lincoln County, Missouri girls came down with the disease circa September 1846, a pathogenic mystery because they had traveled nowhere and seen no infected persons. It's likely they caught it from a book that had been mailed to them. In turn, they unwittingly infected the neighborhood.

In May 1857, an elderly pox victim named Markham was abandoned by the side of the road in Palmer, Massachusetts, where he remained helpless for days in the broiling heat. After he was rescued and taken to a hospital, he explained that he was from Wilbraham and when he came down with the disease, the town's overseer of the poor hauled him to Palmer and dumped him.

John Jackson faced a Brooklyn judge on January 12, 1858, on a charge of beating his wife. He had just been pronounced guilty when bystanders noticed that Jackson was breaking out with a virulent strain of smallpox—right there in court! People bounded for the doors, some of whom merely thought the building was on fire. The clerk somersaulted out a window at great risk of breaking his neck. He was followed by the judge. The deputy sheriff and other officers climbed the pillars and hid in the rafters. Some hardy soul kicked Jackson out the door and told him never to return.

For several years during and after the Civil War, communities were plagued by guerrilla raids. But that was no problem in Cloverport, Kentucky, in December 1864. True, seventeen citizens had died of smallpox within three weeks and fifty more were infected. But at least it scared Confederate guerrillas away.

In their panic, people performed many disrespectful acts against the dead. When a Black woman died of smallpox in Limestone County, Alabama, circa March 1866, everyone was afraid to retrieve her body and give it a proper burial. The owner of the house where she died urged the agent of the Freedman's Bureau to take the body. Agent Coman offered workers ten dollars per day and expenses—no meager sum at the time—to bury the body, but all refused.

After Harvey Meadows died of the disease in Bolivar, Tennessee, in March 1872, his house was burned to the ground, including all the furniture and bedding within.

A young man staying at a Cadiz, Ohio hotel became ill with smallpox in September 1871. Nervous citizens entered the room, sewed him up in the blanket, smuggled him out the back window, placed him in a wagon, drove him to an abandoned house in the country and left him there with a nurse. The youth died of the pox, possibly exacerbated by exposure, since rain fell into the roofless house. As he was being buried like a mongrel in an open field, neighbors shot at the gravediggers. The nurse was ordered to leave town or be shot.

In June 1872, a woman named Butler, who lived a mile south of Unionville, New York, was stricken. Neighbors abandoned her in a hut at Wantage, New Jersey, near the Wallkill River. No one would look after her, and it appeared she would die alone. An elderly man finally agreed to undertake the task for $25. After she died on a Friday, her attendant threw a quilt over her and fled to the mountains as though pursued by a catamount. The body remained unburied for three days, and the authorities did their job only after residents threatened to prosecute them. During this delay, however, dogs and cats entered the hut and ate sections of the departed, making people worry they would catch the disease via their pets. A man agreed to bury Mrs. Butler for $150. For this sum, he merely dug a hole by the hut and tumbled the body into it, likewise her clothing and furniture from the hovel where she died.

In January 1873, two men with smallpox were put off a steamboat at Madrid Bend, Kentucky. Said a newspaper, "The citizens were afraid to go near them. They were without shelter, food, or medicine, and of course died neglected and alone. The hogs had partially devoured them."

On April 4, 1872, a New York man who suspected he had smallpox expired from fear.

The residents of Ennis, Texas, shot an infected woman in January 1873 rather than allow her to enter town.

The population of Cannelton, Indiana, was so wiped out by the disease in the winter of 1872 that no one dared hold a funeral. A mass ceremony for the dead was held in May 1873.

A man died of smallpox at the Brownsville, Tennessee fairgrounds in the hot weather of May 1873. No one would touch him, and a few days later, everyone fled the neighborhood—not only because of the disease, but also because the summer heat exacerbated decomposition and smelled up the entire area.

Joseph Haughbee and John Pinson died at Evansville, Indiana, of smallpox in 1873, and their remains were brought to Hawesville, Kentucky, for burial in February 1874. But first there was public debate about whether their bodies should be accepted.

So *that's* how afraid our ancestors were of smallpox. Now that the scene is set, let us return to the Louisville jail. As mentioned, it was the location of an outbreak in the late summer of 1872. Tom Smith's fellow prisoner Henry Peyton, convicted of killing a man named Krull in 1870, came down with it. He was taken to the city pesthouse, where persons with communicable diseases recovered or died. Peyton did the latter in September. A week later, another convict, George Vincent, who had killed a man at Anchorage on July 4, 1872, caught the disease and died at the pesthouse.

Some citizens considered this no coincidence. Was the removal of murderers via smallpox a special dispensation of Providence? The *Courier-Journal* asked on November 29, "Is the smallpox avenging the murdered men, or cheating the hangman of his fees, or simply saving Governor Leslie the trouble of signing a commutation of the sentence?" The paper's reason for asking the rhetorical, and unanswerable, questions was that the day before, Tom Smith showed symptoms of the most dreaded disease of his era. Like his predecessors, he was taken to the pesthouse to await his possible end. Dr. Henry D. Pope, jailhouse physician, examined Smith on Thanksgiving morning and declared his patient positive for smallpox. His opinion was seconded by a Dr. Forrester. Jailer Ambrose Camp sent two guards to keep a close eye on Smith.

But it was not close enough. The pesthouse was less securely fortified than the prison. Sometime in the night, Smith escaped by leaping from a second-story window as the guards slept, to the deep mortification of the city's prison authorities. While Louisville was not pleased at having a convicted murderer on the loose, even worse was the incipient smallpox panic. The fear mounted despite early rumors that Smith faked the disease. "If it should turn out that the Negro did not have the smallpox but feigned the symptoms…all in order to make his escape, he has accomplished one of the shrewdest and boldest tricks ever attempted by any criminal to evade the just penalty of the law. It is dangerous for such a man to be at liberty," remarked the *Courier-Journal*.

Smith was seen at the fairgrounds on the afternoon of November 30. The *Courier-Journal* ran a description of Smith on December 1, ostensibly so lawmen could find him but also so everyone else could avoid him. The fugitive was recaptured two days later in the forest area called the Wet Woods on the Seventh Street Road. Realizing the futility of escape when surrounded by officers, he laughed, "Well, boys, here I am again." Smith was in perfect health and of ordinary appearance, proving that the rumors were true. He admitted feigning smallpox by smearing croton oil on his face.

Croton oil is still marketed but seldom used because it is expensive and, if swallowed, causes (in rising order of seriousness) mouth burning, dizziness, death and diarrhea. But if applied externally, it causes swelling, irritation and pustules and makes the skin slough off—in other words, it mimics the look of a bad case of smallpox. Very few persons were willing to get close enough to a faker to see whether the symptoms were authentic. Evidently, this trick was known to the nineteenth-century criminal element (see my book *Horror in the Heartland* for another example). Smith likely got the idea after his fellow prisoners died of smallpox. But how did he get croton oil in jail? That was the big question. An assistant must have smuggled it to him, but whom? Hot rumors were afoot, as the *Courier-Journal* acknowledged on December 5: "The most startling stories are afloat in regard to the manner of his escape, but we forbear publishing them until better authenticated."

Dr. Pope, who had declared Smith's malady genuine, was one of the most embarrassed professional men in the city. A *Courier-Journal* reporter tried to soothe his discomfort in the December 4 issue by writing something along the lines of, *Oh well, two other men died of smallpox just before Smith supposedly came down with it, so what else could Dr. Pope have expected?*

On December 12, a couple of weeks after Smith's adventure, a real smallpox victim was refused admittance to the pesthouse. An investigation was called for, then never mentioned again. Perhaps the proprietors, having been so badly burned, were warier than they should have been.

Tom Smith's petition to the court of appeals for a retrial, filed months earlier, was rejected. His daring jailbreak did not help his plea for clemency. On January 21, 1873, the deputy sheriff had the unpleasant task of reading the governor's death warrant to the prisoner, which gave March 28 as the scheduled date of the execution. The deputy was far more emotional than Smith, who calmly declared he was innocent but thought hanging would beat a long prison sentence.

Ten days before the hanging, a reporter checked in on Smith. For the second time, he asserted his innocence. Men who well knew their craft constructed the gallows on March 27 in a section of town between Fourteenth and Fifteenth Streets whimsically called California. The *Courier-Journal* described the contraption in the same sort of thorough detail we use to describe a new sports car to envious friends. The site was only a couple hundred yards from where William Kriel had been hanged in 1870 for shooting his wife. Smith solemnly reiterated his guiltlessness, providing a reporter with a lengthy list of reasons why he couldn't have murdered Breeden. He concluded, "It's not likely that I'd stand here and tell a falsehood. It's too late for falsehoods now. My time's pretty short."

The day before he paid the law's penalty, Tom Smith gave a *Courier-Journal* reporter a protracted interview. The "cheerful" prisoner covered a range of subjects, including his place of birth (Logan County) and age (about twenty-eight), and said that he was the former slave of Samuel Duncan. But his innocence was his favorite topic, and he blamed his plight on Mrs. Breeden, an Officer Butler (whom he accused of perjury) and a detective called "Yankee" Bligh: "A man in the fix I am would not tell a lie.…I will die a man who was innocently hung.…I am not guilty, and I tell you now I never did but one crime in Kentucky, and that was to take some bacon I knew to be stolen and sell it for another man."

Of course, reporters wanted to know how he got that croton oil with which he made his pesthouse escape. Tom knew they would ask and had a fellow prisoner write an account on his behalf, since Smith was illiterate. It was a long document, but the upshot was that he had obtained it from Dr. Pope, the jailhouse physician. According to Smith's version, the suspicious Pope had asked, "What do you want with it?" Smith honestly replied, "I want to put it on my breast so I can go to the pesthouse." Pope promised to acquire it for a fifty-dollar bribe. Smith had only thirty-four dollars, but he raised the rest by gambling with cellmates. Then Dr. Pope raised his price to seventy-two dollars, and Smith had no choice but to come up with the rest of the amount. Later, Smith said, he was offered inducements by various friends of the doctor to keep his story to himself, but he virtuously denied all overtures. He told reporters who questioned his story, "I shall die sticking to what I say.…I am about to die and I would not want to harm any man, but this is the truth."

Smith insisted that while he did not kill the shopkeeper Breeden, he was present when it happened and knew the real killer's identity. Strangely, he told no one this until his time had nearly run out. He ended the interview touchingly, asking the newsmen to make sure his wife did not suffer from poverty, as she would soon have no one to support her.

A week before the execution date, Judge Bruce sent Governor Leslie a telegram beseeching him to commute Smith's sentence to life imprisonment— and if not that, Bruce asked a little desperately, could Smith at least have one more week of life? The governor had a reputation for being a softy when it came to pardons and commutations, so the prisoner and his defenders had high hopes. But Leslie could see no reason to interfere with the verdict and sent back a terse refusal.

On his final morning, March 28, Smith's sickly wife visited him. Their goodbye was very moving. Before he left his cell, Smith had someone draft a letter to the *Courier-Journal's* editor in which he stoutly proclaimed his innocence half a dozen more times and complained that he found no justice because "I was a poor black man, friendless, penniless, and alone." A little after noon, Smith emerged from jail accompanied by Sheriff Thomas Shanks, his deputies and seventy-eight officers; even this mighty show of force had difficulty keeping back the many thousands of gawkers who choked the streets stretching from Jefferson to Seventh. Kentucky was, in 1873, one of the few states that still held public executions.

Smith rode to the scaffold in a furniture van. One witness at the site was the widowed Mrs. Breeden, who observed it all from a carriage. Even at the foot of the gallows stairs, Smith maintained his innocence. As he prayed, he blamed and forgave everyone simultaneously: "Forgive Governor Leslie for not giving me only one week more, for he thought he was right! Forgive Mr. Shanks, the sheriff, for he knows he is right! Forgive all them that swore falsely against me! Have mercy, my God, for I'm innocent! I only wanted one week more, one week, and they wouldn't give it to me!"

But after standing on the trapdoor a few moments, Smith decided it was in his best interest to come clean. He surprised everyone—okay, a few people—by confessing that he was guilty of murdering Breeden after all, something that appears to have been doubted by no one except his attorneys and ministers. "My God, forgive me!" he shouted. "I killed that poor man!" Had Smith not finally told the truth, he would have given his jurors sleepless nights for years. He also admitted that he had lied when he said Officer Butler bore false testimony against him.

But how about that croton oil? In literally his last moments, Smith clarified that "a very poor person, a good friend of mine" gave him the croton oil, but that Dr. Pope furnished it: "Dr. Pope knew all about it." After he spoke, the black hood was placed over his head, the noose looped around his neck and his legs tied. The trap opened at 12:21 p.m.

If some in the crowd were secretly hoping for a ghastly spectacle, they got one. Tom Smith's neck was not instantly broken, and his body convulsed for several minutes. Then the struggle ended. Twenty minutes after the trapdoor opened, Smith was pronounced dead—ironically, by Dr. Pope.

The day after the execution, the *Courier-Journal* ran a melodramatic anti–death penalty poem by "M.P.B." on its front page. The idea behind "Expiation" was to draw a parallel between the deaths of victim Breeden and killer Smith. The final lines:

> *Strangled! This is the law;*
> *And, being so, law is murder.*

It was a noble (and strangely modern) effort at moral equivalence, but M.P.B. was unable to see the difference between a murder committed against an innocent person out of greed and an execution perpetrated by the state, for the defense of its citizens, against a guilty party. In the same issue, the newspaper ran a lengthy editorial expressing sympathy for Tom Smith while admitting the penalty was just and proper since his confession removed all doubt of his responsibility and because the most serious possible crime deserved the most serious possible punishment. But certainly, the writer conceded, better methods of executions must be found and executions should not be held in public.

Ordinarily that would be the end of the story, but not this time. There was still that croton oil business to clear up. Dr. Pope addressed a note to the public, printed in the *Courier-Journal* on March 30, demanding that the county levy court (a court that performs functions usually undertaken by county commissioners) investigate Tom Smith's charges to clear his reputation as a doctor and an honest man. In the same issue, the clearly nervous newspaper fulsomely, obsequiously praised the doctor: "It is sufficient to say that no man stands higher in his profession and in the opinion of those who are acquainted with him; and we have no doubt that the ordeal through which he proposes to pass himself will prove in every way honorable to him. We credit not one word of the Negro's statement."

Dr. Pope got his wish. The court opened an investigation, which wrapped up on May 10. The findings were reported four times in the May 21 *Courier-Journal*: he was "exonerated entirely." The March 30 edition had made the same claim three times even before the inquiry was launched, all of which suggests the paper feared a libel suit as much as the average citizen feared a smallpox patient's sneeze. The court's official statement was that Pope did not provide Smith with the croton oil, did not know he had slathered his face with it, was not neglectful when the prisoner obtained the foul stuff and was not incompetent when he thought Smith had a genuine case of smallpox. The comprehensiveness of this legalistic groveling additionally hints that someone, somewhere was trying to stave off a lawsuit.

Was the physician satisfied with his multiple public vindications? He was not. On May 23, the newspaper published a long letter from Pope in which he complained that his relations with the officials at the jail where he worked had been "most unpleasant" since Smith's accusation—especially jailer Ambrose Camp, who had believed Smith. Pope said Camp was conspiring to ruin him and had even tried to stop the investigation into Smith's charges. Pope charged that Camp had encouraged the prisoner to lie about the doctor's role in the smallpox hoax. *Now that I have been acquitted*, said Dr. Pope, *I'm going to find out who originated the slander, and I'm gonna make him pay!*

This was followed, on May 25, by an even longer public letter by jailer Camp in which, to put it briefly, he denied all of Pope's charges. Camp attached a separate letter supporting his version of events, written by a Joseph G. Wilson. The next day, the *Courier-Journal* printed Camp's entire production a second time, including the Wilson addendum, presumably out of concern that readers might have missed seeing it the day before. Nothing more was heard from Dr. Pope, so I guess Camp won the publicity battle, although Pope had a moral victory when the court cleared his name.

Had a bottle of croton oil ever caused so much trouble?

Chapter 18

EVERYTHING LOOKS LOVELIER

BY CANDLELIGHT

The press couldn't agree whether Jacob's surname was Daub or Doup, but that was of small importance. What mattered was that on the afternoon of October 16, 1873, dairyman Daub shot his wife through the head in their backyard on Rowan Street. Daub, a forty-five-year-old German immigrant, got drunk afterward. His son John came home from work a few hours later and saw his father sitting on the porch with a double-barreled rifle in hand. Jacob Daub spoke. The papers don't record what he said— probably something like "Howdy, son, how was work?" He did not trouble to explain the gun.

John entered the two-room frame cottage and noticed his mother, Dorothy, lying on a blood-soaked mattress in the yard. The poor woman's brains were scattered a considerable distance. He fled and informed the neighbors, who came to investigate but, after seeing an armed Jacob Daub, decided this was business best left to the police. Officers Trainor, Wyatt and Pickering approached and found Daub sleeping on the porch. They disarmed him and woke him up. Daub readily admitted his guilt. He said that his wife had been unfaithful and really, he should have killed her years before.

What was the mattress doing in the backyard? Mrs. Daub had been shucking corn so she could stuff the mattress with husks when her husband sneaked up behind her with his shotgun. At least she never knew what happened. The Daubs' neighbors figured that since the killer was safely in custody, they might as well enter the yard and partake of that singular thrill one gets when seeing a shotgunned corpse in the early stages of rigor mortis.

By then, it was sundown, so several brought candles so as not to miss a single detail. They got a spectacle when the coroner moved the body and they could see that the back of Mrs. Daub's head was mangled and she had an exit wound in her face that probably inspired many to ask forgiveness for their sins that night. After the body was removed, eyewitnesses eagerly told latecomers what they just missed seeing.

Persons who knew the Daubs testified before the coroner's jury. They had kind words for the victim but agreed that Jacob was abusive. Mrs. Raini, the next-door neighbor, said she often heard Jacob threaten to kill his wife.

After sobering up and realizing what trouble he was in, Daub cut his throat in his cell on October 20. He recovered enough to go on preliminary trial on November 6. There wasn't much of a defense, nor could there have been. Jacob's malevolence toward his wife was long-standing and well attested, he was found with the gun in his hand and he freely admitted guilt when the officers rousted him from his slumber. The verdict was that Daub must be tried for murder when the next term of the circuit court began on May 4, 1874.

Daub's case was delayed until November 1874, but he became ill several weeks beforehand, so it was delayed again until February 1875. But he would not live to see trial. His sickness worsened, and the symptoms became horrifying. Paralysis struck both legs, then extended to his bladder and bowels, to the arms and, finally, his mouth. In his last days, he was unable to swallow.

Daub died miserably on December 5, 1874. His tortures were mental as well as physical; all the time he was in prison, he was haunted by visions of his wife's death. Thomas Smith and his smallpox-faking caper must have made a long-lasting local impression, since Daub's obituary notes: "Dr. Pope called in eminent physicians to consult with him. It is therefore no croton oil case."

Chapter 19

MURDERS-IN-LAW

It was just before Christmas, December 23, 1871. Widow Nannie Klanner, age sixty-five, lived in the Germantown neighborhood, but on this date, she was visiting her son, thirty-seven-year-old butcher Charles Weisert, who lived on Cane Street. There was not even a hint of trouble or bad feeling between Nannie and Weisert's family. At four o'clock, she told her son she was ready to go home, so he went to the stable to hitch his horse to a wagon.

Charles was gone only a few minutes, but when he returned, he saw his mother lying on the floor in a pool of blood. His wife, Elizabeth, was sitting on the woman's body and belaboring her head with a hatchet while holding her youngest child with her other hand. She stopped only when her husband approached. Then she sprang off the body and aimed a blow at Charles. She missed, and he seized the weapon.

Elizabeth, age thirty-two, fled to the house of a neighbor, where she was arrested within minutes. Meanwhile, Charles found that his mother was still alive. A doctor was called in and dressed the wounds, for all the good that could have done. Nannie died at her son's home on December 26.

No one could fathom the motive. Officer Rupp, who arrested Elizabeth, said she was always quiet and peaceable and that Nannie Klanner had always seemed to get along with the entire family. On the way to jail, Elizabeth protested, "When my mother and two sisters were poisoned fourteen years ago, nothing was said about it. Now I'm being arrested because I killed the old woman." A *Courier-Journal* reporter who saw Elizabeth at the station house described her cloudy thought processes. She professed to have no idea why she had been arrested and, when told, asked, "Did I hurt my mother-in-law?" The reporter replied that she most certainly had, and Elizabeth could not noodle that one out, remarking that she had always been on good terms with the older lady. But after a while, she muttered darkly, "She did not treat me right. She did not treat me with proper respect."

That was as much of a motive as anyone ever learned, but the lack of insight did not prevent journalists from pointing at what they thought the real cause: insanity, triggered by trashy novels—the "effects of bad reading," said the *Courier-Journal*. Elizabeth devoured German novels featuring suicides, murders and poisonings and lurid, blood-besotted magazines. She especially liked publications that were extravagantly illustrated with "the most suggestive style of art." By "suggestive," the paper meant gore, not smut. The *Courier-Journal* recommended summarily suspending the First Amendment, at least for purveyors of such trash. "The illustrations of horrible crimes which disgrace every page are only too apt to awaken the latent devil in a brutal or semi-idiotic mind," editorialized the paper, before approvingly noting that recently, in one New York town, sellers of such magazines were indicted and fined for inciting crime. "If the publishers are not, or cannot be punished, the people, who are the sufferers, have to resort to another means of relief," warned the paper.

A person blessed with sarcasm, the greatest of gifts, might have observed that the *Courier-Journal*'s initial coverage of the murder was quite graphic itself. Sample line from the first report: "In the middle of the floor, weltering in her life-blood, lay [Charles Weisert's] aged mother, stretched at full length and motionless, her head cut and mangled in a most horrible manner, and the brains issuing from the ghastly wounds." If illustrated, it would have been indistinguishable from anything in the latest issue of *Police Gazette*. It should be noted, too, that in 1871, the technology for creating newspaper images was in its infancy. When it was perfected a few years later, the *Courier-Journal* often ran depictions of crimes that competed with drawings from any sleazy novel.

Mrs. Weisert faced the city court on December 28. An ungentlemanly reporter described her appearance:

> *She has a sallow, melancholy, somewhat hard countenance, with rather prominent features and a restless eye. The face is not of an idiotic stamp, and the forehead is sharp and well-defined, but narrow. Her dress was rather slovenly. She wore one of the old-fashioned looking hood bonnets, commonly worn in this city by women belonging to the working classes.*

The reader might be wondering why the reporter troubled to describe the shape of her forehead. In 1871, science was enthralled by the theory of atavism, which held that criminals or the insane were less advanced-looking than the rest of the population and that they were throwbacks to an earlier time in the development of man. It was believed that a felon could be detected by his appearance, and the more apelike he looked, the more pronounced his insanity or criminal tendencies. Rare is the newspaper account of a late-nineteenth-century murderer that doesn't wax profound over the bumps on his head, the size of his jaw, whether his eyes are too close together and so on. In this case, the journalist was surprised that Mrs. Weisert didn't have a brow that portended evil.

Mrs. Weisert's attorney, Humphrey Marshall, thought his client should be confined in a "proper place" such as a hospital or infirmary, not a prison cell. Prosecutor Hagan replied that since she had hatchet-murdered an inoffensive human, she ought to remain in jail: "What is meant by sending her to a proper place? I don't know anywhere else she should be sent by this court." The judge returned her to her cell, isolated from other prisoners and with medical attention. The reporter who covered the proceedings ended: "There seems to be very little doubt that the woman's intellect has been impaired by poring over the vicious publications of the day, with their horrible details and illustrations of crimes of all kinds, and by insatiate reading of cheap novels and other evil literature."

Elizabeth Weisert did not stay in jail long. Her husband paid her bail, and by the turn of the New Year, she was confined to the city hospital. She was tried on January 13, 1872, found insane and sent to the state asylum at Lexington. The physician there wrote a letter in early April stating that Mrs. Weisert was as badly off as ever, and in his opinion, she would never recover her senses. The record is silent as to her fate, but she must have died in the asylum within a few years, since Charles married Caroline Smith on December 27, 1877. Maybe his second wife wasn't a lunatic.

ON THE LAST DAY of the year 1873, carpenter John B. Parker of New Albany, Indiana, thought it important to shoot his wife, Clara, and himself. Before doing so, he advised her, "Pray and prepare for death." Clara survived; he didn't. At least let's hope he didn't, because they buried him. Parker's deed may have inspired another that took place across the river in Louisville two days later.

Thomas Cooke (or Cook) was already known to the police as a hard case. On the morning of August 22, 1873, someone set fire to a ropewalk and four frame buildings, formerly used as stables by the government during the Civil War, at the Oakland racecourse three miles from the city. A Black family was killed, consisting of Caroline Willis and her children Laura, Bob, Ad and Nina; the father, Squire Willis, died on August 26. Cooke was arrested as the suspected arsonist, but there was no hard evidence, and he was released. "From these and other crimes committed at intervals during the past six years, he has become notorious as being one of the most hardened, vindictive, and daring desperados that are known by the police and community of Louisville," said the *Courier-Journal*.

In 1870, Cooke was so foolish as to marry a woman named Mary, a.k.a. Mollie, described as "a beautiful harlot." As a reporter gently worded it, "It seems to be the universal opinion in the neighborhood that during this period, she had given proof to him and the community that she was not as constant to him as their marriage vow had promised." She also had a reputation for leading young women down the same primrose path, which suggests that she had a side career as a minor league madam, procurer, pimp, pimpette or whatever term you wish to employ.

Thus Cooke's jealousy was constantly agitated. To say their domestic life was inharmonious would be an understatement. As recently as December 19, 1873, Mary had gone to the cops out of fear that her abusive husband might kill her. But Tom played nice when the police came calling and so fooled them.

Cooke's breaking point came when his wife attended a New Year's Eve ball without him, at a place known to be frequented by prostitutes, rowdies and "fast young men." Cooke had long suspected that his mother-in-law, Marilla Rutledge, encouraged his wife's behavior ("an abettor of her daughter's shame," to use the press's phrase).

His temper was not assuaged the next day, January 2, 1874, when Mrs. Rutledge gave him what-for: "Tom, if you can't behave yourself, you must leave the house, and I tell you now to go and never come here again." Cooke bid the Deity to drat them, or something along those lines, and drew a Barlow knife from his pocket. He stabbed Mary in the back five times; sank the knife deeply into his mother-in-law's breast, back and shoulder; and after scaring away a young friend of Mrs. Cooke's named Ellen Martin, carved an unattractive five-inch gash in his own throat.

When the coroner arrived, Cooke, believing he was dying, made a full confession—which meant that if he survived, he would likely be imprisoned or hanged for murder. A reporter described the appearances of the slasher and his wife, as readers would expect nothing less. Cooke was slightly built, with a light moustache and black hair. The reporter noted with surprise, "His general appearance is not that of the desperado," because it was thought that criminals were supposed to look like criminals (see description of Mrs. Weisert, earlier). Mary Cooke, meanwhile, was "very handsome," with black eyes, black hair and a "rounded form" (you figure it out) that "rendered her attractive to all." But observe: no description of poor Mrs. Rutledge.

On January 4, the *Courier-Journal* acknowledged that the horrifying tale sold papers, making its earlier criticism of blood-and-thunder literature seem hypocritical: "The morning papers were eagerly read to obtain the minutest details. Everything that pertained to the affair was eagerly devoured, all other news being of trifling import." Naturally, hundreds of people trooped to see the house on Shelby Street. They would have been less than human if they hadn't. A score of Lafayette Street cyprians came to console the wounded Mary Cooke, their "sister in sin." A lot of men came to see her too—a *lot*. One was James Garley, supposedly the man whose attentions to Mary finally caused Tom to blow his stack.

Surprisingly, both husband and wife survived. At first, Mr. Cooke seemed to be not only at death's door but also wiping his feet on death's doormat, which is only polite, but he was sound enough to be taken to jail the day after the murderous assault. A throng watched as he was lifted from his bed into the covered wagon that carried him away, like Hamlet, the observed of all observers. Many followed it on foot, and others stopped whatever they were doing to watch as the conveyance passed down the street. Mary Cooke's health was further jeopardized by an inflammation. Doctors wanted to take her to City Hospital, but she refused. As for Mrs. Rutledge, she was borne to the frozen sod of Western Cemetery.

The grand jury indicted Tom Cooke for murder on January 20. The trial was held in Shepherdsville, Bullitt County, on September 28. Cooke and his attorneys had few options, since he had confessed when erroneously thinking he was about to pass forever from the glories of life and Louisville. He was found guilty on September 30, but the sentence was scandalous—merely five years in prison for stabbing his wife five times and killing his mother-in-law. A thunderstruck newspaper correspondent wrote, "To everyone who remembers the particulars of the horrible affair on Shelby Street, it will be a matter of astonishment, as well as curiosity, to know how an intelligent and enlightened jury could return such a verdict, if no improper motives caused it." (That last sentence meant the reporter speculated that the jury may have been bribed.) To put the outrage in perspective, not long before, common burglars in Shepherdsville had received sentences of six to ten years. Despite this leniency, Cooke's attorneys thought they could do better and vowed they would file for a retrial. Whether they got a second trial I do not know, but Tom certainly was in prison as of May 1876, when he made headlines for trying to stab Sam South, one of his keepers at Frankfort prison. It was a habit with him.

Mary fully recovered and became a noted "woman of the town" (prostitute, that is), still blessed with those good looks and that "rounded form." In November 1875, she did something that, in the community's eyes, likely was far worse than being a harlot: she ran off to Cincinnati with a nineteen-year-old stage actor/juggler. The happy couple had met at a prostitute ball on Jefferson Street. The pair was said to be preparing to marry in Baltimore. Nothing bad could possibly come of this. Yes?

As for that unsolved arson of which Thomas Cooke was suspected: his brother Charles went on trial for it on January 19, 1874, but was discharged, as had been Thomas, for lack of evidence.

Chapter 20

SWEENEY AND FENN BEG TO DIFFER

Mrs. DeVoto, who also went by the name Louisa Ragsdale (or Ragsdall), was strolling near the corner of Louisville's Chestnut and Preston Streets on a long-ago day in 1857 Louisville. The ensuing unpleasant event was kept out of the papers at first, but most likely it occurred on March 30. Her escort was foundry worker Casper Fenn, age twenty-two, stout and powerfully built. They were followed by John Sweeney, a dissolute and armed young man. Fenn and Sweeney got into an argument about something, probably the question of who had the right to Mrs. DeVoto's company. Witnesses said Fenn pointed at his adversary and said, "If you follow me further, I'll knock you down." Fenn then smiled a probably insincere smile and said something inaudible. That was the last thing he ever did.

The inquest was held March 31. The principal finding was that Fenn died of two pistol shots to the thorax.

"Murder Trial" was the headline in the *Courier* of October 16, along with the confident assertion that Sweeney would be tried in criminal court that very day. But he wasn't. Sweeney bided his time in jail for an entire year, making the improving and character-building acquaintance of six others accused of murder.

The trial began at last on October 15, 1858. The defense claimed that Fenn had threatened Sweeney earlier on the day of the murder for spending time with Mrs. DeVoto and, to further register his displeasure, had kicked Mrs. DeVoto in her room and ripped the earrings from her ears. (The newspapers made certain to mention that this occurred in her room, likely to discreetly inform readers that she and Sweeney had been up to something in there.) Yet she had gone on a nighttime stroll with Fenn a few hours later. Perhaps unwillingly? Under oath, Mrs. DeVoto claimed Fenn tried to hit Sweeney with a rock.

So Sweeney was a thug who was quick to shoot, or Fenn was a bully, or some combination thereof. The jurors must have been unsure what to think, as they found Sweeney guilty only of manslaughter, though some initially thought he deserved hanging. The sentence was fixed at six years in the penitentiary.

Sweeney served only a fraction of it. One of the outgoing governor's last acts, at the end of August 1859, was to pardon him. The *Courier* was certain that Sweeney was guiltier than the jury thought, and deserved far greater punishment than he received:

> [Sweeney] *laid in jail eighteen months before his sagacious counsel would venture a trial.…Scarcely ten months have passed, and Gov. Morehead, by virtue of authority badly used, sets him free. We do not know what influence brought it about, nor do we care to know. We are certain that he* [has] *done a great wrong, and that this community owes him no thanks for his ill-advised clemency.*

All in all, one is left with the impression that there was a lot more going on in this murder case, including motive and aftermath, than ever was revealed.

Chapter 21

THE MORGUE, THE MERRIER,

OR GRAVE ERRORS

The Wet Woods was a marshy area in Jefferson County. Though located only seven miles from Louisville near the Third Street Road, it was so remote and uninhabited that it might as well have been in Patagonia. It is the area where Thomas Smith was captured after murdering shopkeeper Joseph Breeden. But five years into the future, another big sensation came, on December 11, 1876. Henry Wilder and son were returning home from an old-fashioned (even then) husking party. As they crossed a field half a mile southeast of the L&N Railroad's Strawberry Station, they found the body of a young White male tangled in the branches of a fallen tree. The ground was considerably chewed up a short distance away, indicating a struggle for life; the right side of the corpse's head was pulverized, indicating cause of death; and a heavy bludgeon made of ash wood lay nearby. The murderer had also cut the unknown man's throat.

These circumstances were sufficiently interesting, but the victim's pants and shoes were also missing, and small footprints suggested that a woman had been at the scene. Detectives put these clues together and considered robbery the motive, but the same evidence, including the suggestion of a fight plus the isolation of the setting, suggests a more colorful motive to this writer and possibly to you as well. At any rate, the corpse was an object of abiding interest to every passerby and soon to every newspaper reader in the city.

The body was taken to a vault in the city's Western Cemetery for temporary storage in hopes that friends or family might identify it. The *Courier-Journal* ran a detailed description of the man and his shabby clothing on December 13. On December 14, Charles Cooper, described as "an honest, good-natured, hard-working colored man," asked the sexton of Western Cemetery to show him the stranger. Cooper thought he knew the body's identity, and when he saw it, he exclaimed "That is Ed Collins, sure."

Collins was twenty-five years old, originally from Galveston and Cooper's fellow laborer on Philip Best's farm, located only a mile and a half southeast of Strawberry Station. Cooper was positive his identification was correct, since he had known Collins well and seen him in the city only two weeks before the body was found. "Yes, I'd know that face anywhere," said Cooper, "and them's the very clothes he used to wear on the farm." Cooper claimed he even recognized the deceased's long socks, which Collins wore when hauling charcoal or hay.

Cooper did more than just identify the body: he had a story to tell. Ed P. Collins had been sweethearts with farmer Best's daughter Mary. Sometime back in the summer, she became pregnant, and her increasingly obvious predicament did not endear Collins to his employer. The young man swore he would marry the girl as soon as he had the financial means. A relative owed Mary fifty bucks, and after she collected, she gave the sum to Collins— who then absconded. The Best family came to the city several times looking for him. Their last search mission was on December 11, the day Henry Wilder and his son found the body.

Detectives interviewed the Bests to see if their version of events matched Cooper's. They agreed that Cooper's description of the body sounded like Collins all right, and they shamefacedly admitted that the story of the seduction was true. The date of the marriage was supposed to be November 26, but Collins had not shown up. He appeared afterward with some excuse for his absence, which did little to restore the family's good opinion of him. A new wedding date was set for December 1. Again he vanished, but this time he had a valid reason no one could hold against him: he had been murdered.

When poor Mary Best heard that her fiancé's body was still open for public viewing in that cold, cold vault in Western Cemetery, she was determined to go see him. She made this saddest of journeys on December 15, accompanied by her parents. Imagine her mixed emotions when they gazed upon the corpse's white, waxy face and found that it was *not* Collins. Her sweetie was alive after all, though she probably wished she could kill him. In addition, her parents said they had never seen the coffin's tenant before in their lives. Collins had indeed skipped out on his responsibilities once and for all, despite his lavish promises. His friends later said he fled for Memphis. The *Courier-Journal* remarked, "It is supposed that he is now in that city, rejoicing over his good fortune in escaping the terrors of murder." And escaping the terrors of matrimony, too. We hear nothing more of the Bests and their dilemma.

Meanwhile, since the vault had been open for a week, thousands of men and women—likely children, too—sauntered by to stare at the corpse. Many muttered, "Gee, he looks familiar," but no one could put a name to the fellow. Hundreds more came to see him the next day, to no avail, and authorities decreed that he would be buried on December 18. Indeed, he would *have* to be.

But the mystery seemed to be solved the day before this, uh, deadline. On December 17, two brothers named Patrick and Thomas Monahan identified the murder victim as their brother Martin, twenty-six, a farmer who had been missing from the city for a year. Martin was, unfortunately, fond of alcohol and too often saved his money and then went on protracted drunken sprees. He was not particular about his acquaintances and enjoyed showing off his money to people. Put all these characteristics together and you have a prime candidate for a murder victim. Fortuitously, a bystander named Ed Coffman overheard the brothers. He lived near Strawberry Station, and on the Monday the body was found, he just happened to have seen two men enter Vaundeville's grocery at the station. One of them answered to the murder victim's description. This man bought a pair of socks and a bottle of whiskey. His companion kept his hat pulled low, as though trying to disguise himself. Then they left the store. The Wilders discovered the body a few hours later.

The Monahans were so certain they had found their dearly departed Martin that they took the body—which, by this point, was more than two weeks past its prime and not in spruce condition—to Patrick's house for a funeral. Then, they said, Martin would get a good old Irish wake. A Christian burial in the family plot in the Catholic section of Western Cemetery was planned for the afternoon of December 18.

Their grief lasted only about a week, because who should arrive in Louisville on December 24 but the living, breathing Martin Monahan? He had heard that he was supposed to be dead and came to set the record straight. He had been working on the Robert Mills farm on Floyds Fork for the past three months. When he dropped by Sam Hays's grocery, Hays was startled to see a supposed dead man standing before him—and purchasing whiskey at that—and informed his customer that he was badly wanted in Louisville.

Martin trudged through a snowstorm to get to his brother Tom's house. By the time he got there, the occupants were asleep. He rapped on the door anyway.

"Who is there?" asked Mrs. Monahan.

"It is me," replied Martin.

"Who are you?" asked Tom Monahan.

"Your brother Martin."

"O Lord! It is his spirit!" cried Mrs. M.

Tom cautiously opened the door, and Martin stepped in. "Where in the name of the blessed St. Patrick did you come from?" demanded Tom.

"Well, Tom, you buried me, but I thought I'd just get up again."

But this was no time for levity! Mrs. Monahan was beside herself with terror until Martin explained his previous whereabouts. It turned out to be a Christmas to remember.

What of Ed Coffman's story that seemed to identify Martin Monahan as the victim? His story was a bit too perfect. By sheer coincidence, to hear him tell it, he had seen the victim in company with his killer, who was dressed like a stage villain, and—again by chance—Coffman happened to be on the scene two weeks later when the Monahan brothers saw the body in the crypt. One concludes that the unfolding story in the newspapers appealed strongly to Coffman's ample imagination and he wanted to play a role in it.

A new problem: what should be done with the total stranger lying in the grave purchased by the brothers Monahan in the mistaken belief that he was Martin? The coroner said he had no legal powers to evict the body, and unless the church ordered it removed to a potter's field, it might slumber forever under the name Martin Monahan.

The church did so order, and the stranger was exhumed on December 27. Sophia Stewart attended, thinking the corpse might be her missing son John. It wasn't. The murder victim was returned to the vault at Western Cemetery, but his homecoming was not peaceful. Although he had been dead nearly a month, officials said his body would be kept on display in the vault five more days, but if the winter weather warmed up, forget it. You might be wondering why the authorities hadn't just taken a photo of the body while it was still presentable. The *Courier-Journal* wondered the same.

Did citizens continue to get in line to see the rapidly decaying mystery man? You bet they did, and by the hundreds, on December 28. Charles Cooper studied the face and declared again, against all evidence to the contrary, that he was still convinced it was Ed Collins. About a dozen people had good reason to be there—persons who were missing loved ones of roughly the age and reported description of the murder victim, who hoped to settle the matter at last. Many of the others just wanted a morbid thrill. Everyone had a theory. Some thought it was Collins after all, never mind that he was known to be in Memphis. One man thought it was a Louisville youth who had gone to New York three months before to settle an estate and who must have been waylaid by thieves on his return home. Another thought it was a hobo he had spied on the corner of Ninth and Broadway the day before the murder. Yet another theory, which gained several supporters, held that he was a dues collector for the National Granger movement.

Mrs. Limebaugh, proprietor of a Sixth Street boardinghouse, thought he was a missing schoolteacher who had rented a room. She saw him last two days before the murder. He had said he was going to the country but never returned. She still possessed his trunk but refused to divulge the man's name until more proof emerged. On January 4, 1877, J.Z. Miller, superintendent of the Louisville Employment Agency, identified the missing man as Robert P. Templeton, a Pennsylvanian who had moved to the city in June 1876. Mrs. Limebaugh and one of her tenants, a young lady named Miss Brown, both scrutinized the man in the vault and agreed it was Templeton and no other.

But the Granger man turned up alive, and no one ever proved it was Templeton. It was a singular case of a dead guy who looked like everybody, having been mistaken for Ed Collins, Martin Monahan, the dues collector and possibly Robert P. Templeton. Whoever he was, he was buried once and for all on January 4, his identity known only to God.

Chapter 22

A FORMER SLAVE FINDS FRIENDS

Wagon driver Henry Croomes (name also given as Cooms and Coomes), thirty-four, occupied the middle room of a three-room cottage at the corner of Sixteenth and Gallagher. He shared the place with his twenty-five-year-old girlfriend Emma Chinn, who was also his washerwoman; both were African American. The press saw a moral lesson to trumpet: they "lived in sin" by pretending to be husband and wife. "[O]f course, such a connection is full of quarrels and vicissitudes. Married life is tame as compared with unlawful wedlock: dissensions and bitter jealousies always characterize the latter."

Their dwelling had no privacy. Thin partitions laughably called "walls," which separated the three rooms, were made of boards so loose they provided no protection against prying neighbors. The following is one version of the events that happened on December 9, 1877; another side will be told later.

Croomes and Chinn had an argument just after midnight. Elderly Sallie Belt and her daughter Lizzie, who lived in another section of the house, evidently wanted to see the fight and peeped through a chink in the partition. They saw Chinn lying in bed with her three-year-old daughter. "Get out of that bed and get up here," commanded Henry.

"Henry, I am sick and sleepy," she replied. "Let me alone. I don't want to get up."

Henry brandished a lit coal-oil lamp. "If you won't get up, I'll *make* you get up," he shouted. Then he threw it at her. Emma did not die instantly, and Henry ignored her cries for help. The last the other tenants saw of him, he was putting on his coat. He and all the neighbors in the house fled the burning building. The conflagration destroyed the house, two adjoining cottages and a next-door brewery stable and nearly killed the neighbors and the three-year-old. Poor Emma was "actually cremated," shuddered a headline.

Eyewitnesses told firemen and police what happened, and Henry was taken to the Twelfth Street station house. It was several hours before the ashes cooled enough to permit the retrieval of Emma Chinn's body. It was "a sickening spectacle," said the press. Croomes's preliminary trial was held on December 12. A court reporter observed "the evidence made out a dead case against him."

The trial for murder and arson came on February 8, 1878. In addition to the Belts, the court heard from Amanda Boyce, the occupant of the cottage's third room, who also overheard the argument, though she didn't witness Croomes tossing the lantern. The case against Croomes seemed overwhelming, but there wasn't any rebuttal testimony, which some deemed unfair to the defendant. He had no one to provide evidence of his innocence, but at least he did have a character witness: Ben C. Weaver, whose wife owned Croomes when he was a slave. It took the jury only half an hour to find Croomes guilty and recommend the death penalty. He was agitated: "His face assumed an expression of agony, his frame convulsed and quivered with terror, and when the officers started to conduct him back to jail, he clutched at the table by which he was sitting and made two efforts to arise from his seat before sufficient strength returned to his quaking limbs to raise him to his feet." Nevertheless, he told a reporter afterward that he would rather be hanged than spend life in prison. And from this point, Croomes maintained a happy disposition that was a wonder to all who beheld him.

Croomes was in serious trouble, judging from some of the headlines he garnered over several months: "Booked for Death," "Doomed to Die," "End of His Rope…Sentenced to Be Irrevocably Hung…Hope Past and Death Prospective," "To Be Hanged." October 4 was chosen to be his final day. Croomes took the news more calmly than the sheriff. The only question was whether the execution would be held privately or in public.

A *Courier-Journal* reporter was permitted to question Henry for the September 19 edition, when it appeared the prisoner had barely more than two weeks of life left. The journalist was sympathetic to Croomes and wrote of Chinn's death, "The deed was done behind a locked door, and unless the witnesses observed his actions through the keyhole, they could not positively be aware of the fact"—forgetting that this was essentially just what they did, peeping through holes in the partition boards. Coolly and calmly, Croomes told his side of the story. He declared the fire was Emma Chinn's fault. She had been filling the lamp with oil but failed to blow out the wick first. He shouted for assistance, but no neighbors came, though at least three were behind those pathetic partitions. Croomes told the reporter that the door was locked and the key was lost, so he spent several minutes looking for a chisel, his girlfriend burning alive all the while. At last, she fell on the bed, which also caught fire. Ten minutes after the blaze started in that tiny room, Henry finally got the door open and escaped with the child, and by then the rest of the cottage was aflame, too. Somehow, this story doesn't quite seem to add up, but it convinced Croomes's attorney, Captain J.J. McAfee, and, eventually, many others.

The prosecution had asserted that neighbors heard an argument through the paper-thin walls just before the explosion, but Croomes denied it. "We had been living on the friendliest terms with nothing whatever to mar our happiness in the least particular, and the night of the fire no harsh or angry words had passed between us. On the contrary, we were chatting pleasantly together when the lamp exploded."

The Belts swore they witnessed Croomes tossing that lamp, but he said they were liars with a vendetta against him: "[I] will deny all knowledge of such a charge as my dying statement. I feel perfectly confident that the charges against me were wholly of a malicious nature. All the property of the persons living in the house was entirely destroyed and knowing that I occupied the room where the fire originated, these accusations were trumped up against me purely out of malice. The Belt family worked up the case against me."

Croomes had two final wishes: "My only desire is that I be buried in Cave Hill beside my mother. It is my wish also that the hanging take place privately if possible."

The reporter spoke with attorney McAfee, who was certain of his client's innocence and fought on his behalf, although he said, "I felt rather reluctant about appearing in his defense, knowing that I would receive no recompense for my services" (hey, at least he was honest about it). McAfee took the case to the court of appeals, which affirmed the verdict. After this disappointment, the attorney took the last step he could take to save Croomes, short of baking him a cake with a file in it: he asked Governor McCreary for a commutation, but as of the interview with the reporter, he had not received a reply.

Before the journalist left the jail, the staff endorsed Croomes. They said he was "one of the quietest and best prisoners that had ever been in the jail."

Could a humble, impoverished former slave accused of a heinous murder find influential friends in this White-oriented, racist society—especially barely a decade after the end of the Civil War? He could and did. Ben Weaver, Croomes's character witness at his trial, published a letter in the September 20 *Courier-Journal* in which he again offered a defense. He pointed out that many in the city, including "some of our best citizens," thought the prisoner was innocent. Weaver hurried affidavits to the governor in Frankfort. Several other powerful persons supported the condemned man. Judge William Jackson, who had sentenced him; commonwealth's attorney Basil Duke, who had prosecuted him; the original jurors; ex–chief justice William Lindsey, who prepared the court of appeals's decision against Croomes—all urged the governor to consider a commutation of the sentence to life in prison, if not an outright pardon.

As October 4 drew closer, Croomes never lost his calm or sunny personality: "When asked if he entertained any hopes of receiving a respite, he said he had no hopes of life, no fear of eternity." He showed people a photograph of his wife, who lived in Nelson County with their four children, and said several citizens, White and Black, had visited his cell and brought treats and flowers. Some sang hymns with him. Many persons were troubled that he would be hanged, although no testimony was given in his favor at his trial, which seemed without precedent.

The *Courier-Journal* noted on October 3, "The advocates of Croomes's innocence say that he went into the trial totally unprepared…so great was his ignorance of the law," though of course it was not Croomes's responsibility to know the workings of the law but rather his lawyer's. The prisoner was "by no means a brute in appearance," said the reporter. (Mark, yet again, that emphasis on the physical appearance of accused criminals, as noted in previous chapters. Would people have been more likely to think Croomes guilty if he had resembled a "brute"?)

On October 3, wagonloads of people from outside Louisville came to see the kind of public exhibition they could not see in a theater. Hotel rooms were booked as though a convention were in town. The scaffold had been constructed near Sixteenth and Kentucky Streets. But somebody did all that hard work for nothing. Governor McCreary sent a message delaying the execution until November 8 so he could again peruse the testimony and evidence.

McCreary's final decision: he commuted the sentence to life imprisonment. Considering the lingering doubt, it was a wise decision. But Croomes's happiness at the news is a matter of conjecture, considering that he once said he preferred hanging to a life term.

Chapter 23

WHEN JURISDICTIONS COLLIDE

Colonel Stephen Ormsby had a farm about nine miles east of the city, an area therefore known as Ormsby's Woods, and on May 16, 1869, one of his workers, a young Black woodcutter named George Polk (also called Pope) disappeared. Constables and searchers unsuccessfully sought Polk, but suspicion built against John Conley, also called Collins, a former soldier in the United States Colored Troops. On May 27, Conley was arrested on suspicion and taken to jail in Louisville. He was released, since there was insufficient evidence, but was arrested again on a charge of incest against his daughter.

The search for Polk continued while Conley was in in jail, and on the last day of May, farm workers discovered the body in a thicket, its head bearing two immense concave wounds. When coroner Moore told the prisoner, Conley hesitated a few moments, then confessed.

Of the two foul crimes attributed to Conley, he was probably innocent of one. While he was in the army, his wife died, leaving five children. After the war, when Conley went to work for Colonel Ormsby, his children lived with him on the premises. He insisted on sleeping in the same room with his eighteen-year-old daughter because Polk and another young man slept in the room above. Conley must not have trusted them. But his other four children also slept with the rest of their family, so if Conley had evil intentions, he didn't have much privacy in which to indulge them.

It appears that Polk resented Conley's attitude about safeguarding his daughter's chastity, because it was he who started the nasty incest rumor that caused the former soldier no end of embarrassment and anger. Gradually, he discovered the gossiper's identity, and on that deadly May 16, he accompanied Polk into the forest on a wood-chopping mission, pretending friendliness all the while. Both carried axes. As they started cutting rail timber, Conley revealed what was really on his mind.

"Why did you circulate that report against me? A man that can tell such a lie is a thief and would rob the grave of his mother. I don't think it's any harm to kill someone who would swear to as big a lie as you did."

Conley later claimed that Polk drew back his axe as if to strike him, saying, "You mustn't talk to me that way, or I'll chop your head off!"

But Conley was quicker, and he felled Polk with a blow to the back of the head with the flat side of his own axe. He hit Polk again in a fury, on the right side of the head this time. It was sufficient. Conley hid the body under a log, where it was not detected for two weeks.

Perhaps it was a spontaneous killing in anger; perhaps it was a coolly calculated murder; perhaps it was a case of self-defense. A convincing argument could be made for any of these possibilities, but the press had already decided that Conley was a demon incarnate. Said one reporter, "When he swings from the gallows, fiends will snatch at his body, and the world will be rid of one of its vilest inhabitants."

The case began in circuit court on November 28. Judge Bruce ruled that Conley's confession could not be used before the jury, since he suspected it was coerced: "Is it not violative of the rule that no confession shall be used against an accused [person] unless freely and voluntarily made?…Had an intelligent, free-born, free-raised man, with the advantages of friends and counsel, been subjected to such an examination, I might have come to a different conclusion."

Of course, other evidence was admissible, and on December 1, a jury found Conley guilty with a recommendation of hanging. Said a reporter: "The conviction was received with ill-concealed satisfaction by all in the courtroom, but especially by the Negroes, who had taken a deep interest in the case from first to last and flocked to the trial by hundreds."

Many Northern newspapers, especially the *New York Tribune*, erroneously complained that the state of Kentucky did not permit Black witnesses to testify at Conley's trial. Remonstrated the *Courier-Journal*'s editorialist:

> *There is no word of truth in the assertion that the Negro, tried recently in Judge Bruce's court, was not allowed to bring forward black witnesses to testify in his case. The witnesses upon all the material points in his case*

were black. He was convicted wholly upon black testimony [true, since his confession was excluded as evidence], *no Negro witness being excluded. There were ten or a dozen Negro witnesses and only two or three white ones, the latter being examined principally upon immaterial points, such as the condition of the murdered man's body, etc. The prisoner was tried for killing a Negro....The Negroes of our state are competent to testify in such cases.*

(On the other hand, Kentucky was the last southern state to permit Blacks to testify against Whites, in the 1872 murder case *Blyew v. United States*, and even then only because the federal government forced the issue.)

On December 5, Conley's attorneys made a motion for a retrial. Judge Bruce warned the prisoner not to get his hopes up, "but to direct his thoughts to another world [as] there is little hope for him in this."

The motion for a second trial was assigned to be heard on February 5, 1869. Those pessimists of the press remarked, "It is pretty well understood that the motion will be overruled, and that Conley will expiate his great offense at the end of a rope in midair." Their opinion seemed well justified on February 27, when Judge Bruce denied the motion and passed Conley's sentence: death by hanging on April 30. Conley was lucky in a way, as many thought he would be executed as early as April 10.

Ten days before his slated doom, Conley was reportedly "perfectly resigned to his awful fate....He is constantly attended by a spiritual advisor of his own race and devotes himself unremittingly to the work of absolution." He told a reporter in an interview published on April 28: "My only regret now is that I cannot read. It would be a great comfort if I could pass the time in reading the Bible....They may destroy this body, but the soul they cannot harm." He expressed sorrow when told his former employer, Colonel Ormsby, had recently died. And he still held out hope for a miracle: "If the pardon comes, all well and good. If not, I am ready for the worst."

And then—the miracle came! Maybe it was the prayers; maybe it was his lawyers' petition to Governor Stevenson; maybe it was some combination thereof. But instead of being hanged on April 30, Conley was respited for another month after the federal government served a writ of mandamus on Sheriff Martin as he supervised the noose-tying, after which the prisoner was placed under the protection of the U.S. district court, not the local courts. Some questioned the legality of the reprieve, as it was first time since the end of the war that a federal court had annulled the proceedings of a Kentucky court. Considering that states' rights was one of the major causes of the conflict, it was still a touchy subject. To put it simply, which authorities had jurisdiction over Conley's fate—state or federal?

The new execution date was May 28, but Conley could not be hanged without the federal court's consent. Just before that date, a motion was made to remand him to the custody of state authorities. They took charge of Conley under a writ of habeas corpus. "The Negro murderer Conley is likely to live through the warm weather," the *Courier-Journal* commented drily, and so he did, after the governor extended his respite to October 29. To cut through the legalese: no one had the slightest idea what to do with Conley, and the state, as embodied by the governor, was trying not to step on the feds' toes.

The two jurisdictions batted Conley's fate back and forth like a badminton birdie. At last, the case was heard by the Supreme Court, which ruled that Kentucky courts had authority. This meant that the original sentence was upheld, and it seemed Conley would be hanged on April 26, 1872, alongside Matthew Shanahan, an Irishman who had murdered C.W. Montgomery in August 1870.

Imagine how Conley felt, having spent nearly three years under the shadow of possibly being hanged. A reporter who saw him after he got the bad news in March 1872 wrote: "He has not seen the sun for a whole year, and has not been absent from the prison, except to attend his trial....His hair is beginning to turn gray, but otherwise he looks young, healthy, strong, and sprightly. He and Shanahan are together every day and console each other in their common misfortune."

And now imagine how Conley felt—and Shanahan, too—when on April 16, Governor Leslie commuted their sentences to life in prison, once and for all. The *Courier-Journal's* Small Talk columnist was glad. "The impecunious double hanging is off," he crowed, and then argued that rich murderers ought to be hanged more often, though in earlier columns he had called the practice un-Christian and barbaric. Was he suggesting that Conley and Shanahan—both unquestionably guilty of murder—should have been given a chance to buy their way out of trouble, and somehow that would have served the ends of justice?

Before being sent away to prison for good, Conley admitted he was guilty of killing George Polk but maintained that the deceased richly deserved it for spreading that lie.

Chapter 24

ATTEMPTED GLAND THEFT

Number 637 South Thirty-Fourth Street looked like a most ordinary dwelling. But no one dwelled there permanently; it was a furnished rented house. And the purpose for which one person rented it sent shock waves through Jazz Age Louisville for many weeks back in the spring of 1924.

On the night of Saturday, March 8, a haggard, terrified man—with good cause to be—staggered out of this address and fled. Passersby noticed that he had handcuffs dangling from one wrist. Police couldn't find him, but in a second-floor back room, they discovered the body of the renter, thirty-three-year-old broker Richard Heaton, whose actual residence was 1315 South First Street—he lived in one house while simultaneously renting another. Heaton, who wore two pistols in shoulder holsters, had been shot to death and was lying with his feet in a closet. That was plenty interesting, but the décor of the room was even more so.

Next to a bedpost, a mattress lay on the floor. It was surrounded by large metal staples driven into the floor. Nearby were surgical tools, bandages, rubber gloves, linen, towels, knives, rubber sheets, chloroform, a bottle of sulfuric acid and operating gowns. Also, a razor-sharp hatchet. And empty boxes. Four pistols in all were found in the house.

In addition to this furniture, detectives found the dead man's widow, Mary Heaton, on the premises. She thought it wise to tell what she knew. Her husband was a friend of the runaway, whose name was William Gates, age thirty-one. William had been the best man at their wedding in 1916.

William Gates, the would-be victim. *Louisville Courier-Journal,* March 9, 1924. *Courtesy of the* Courier-Journal.

Somehow, Richard Heaton had got the idea that she was having an affair with William. Richard stewed over it for four long years, then decided to take the ultimate revenge. All sweetness and false friendliness, he invited William over to his brokerage office in the Board of Trade Building. When William arrived, Richard and two hired men drove him to the rented house. Inside, Richard handcuffed his unsuspecting guest and tied him to the bedpost.

So what was the purpose of the mattress, floor staples and surgical equipment? Well, Mary explained, her husband meant to perform "an operation" on William that the squeamish press was very careful not to name or describe in any detail, but it is clear Richard intended to castrate his perceived rival. The *Courier-Journal* cautiously termed it "a mayhem plot" or "a gland operation" that "would have resulted in his death." It was presumed that after forcing William to undergo this procedure, Richard intended to hack up his body with that hatchet and mail the portions off to distant locations in those boxes.

The press was circumspect as to whether the mutilation was performed, but apparently it wasn't. Instead of getting down to business, Richard left William Gates tied to the bedpost for three days. Perhaps Richard's dawdling was intended to maximize his precious gloating time. But William got free, and after shooting his captor twice, he ran next door to ask a neighbor, R.E. Buscher, to summon a doctor. By chance, Dr. Herbert E. Schoonover happened to be treating a patient in a nearby house and was leaving when Gates approached on the sidewalk and asked for help, saying, "I have shot a man, but don't tell." William added, "I have been a prisoner in that house for three days. I had to do it, doctor." As Schoonover tended to the dying man, William abandoned the neighborhood with a briskness that will provoke the reader's sympathy and understanding. As an illustration of what slaves to fashion we are, he returned to the house of horror to grab his hat and coat before running off into the night.

(Another bizarre aspect of the story is the seemingly disproportionate attention the *Courier-Journal* gave it. It was reported at first in scarehead-sized typeface one generally associates with the outbreak of a world war or a

Above: Gates's mattress. Heaton's body lies at the left in the photo. *Louisville Courier-Journal*, March 9, 1924. *Courtesy of the* Courier-Journal.

Opposite, top: Front view of Heaton's house. *Louisville Courier-Journal*, March 9, 1924. *Courtesy of the* Courier-Journal.

Opposite, bottom: Another view of the death house. *Louisville Courier-Journal*, March 10, 1924. *Courtesy of the* Courier-Journal.

meteoroid headed for Earth. For days, the story was featured on not just the front page but also several inner pages; there were sidebars and interviews with peripheral characters. Lavish photo illustrations depicted the would-be mutilator, the victim, an outer view of the house, the mattress, the room in which Gates was imprisoned and detectives brandishing unpleasant-looking surgical instruments.)

After the news got out, 637 South Thirty-Fourth Street was the most popular place in the city. Naturally! The press called it "the mystery house" and "house of murder," but the name that really stuck was "torture house." Hundreds came to gape at a building they wouldn't have paid the slightest attention to the day before. One proud resident of the street was asked by strangers to recount the story hundreds of times. One may be certain that he

did, and without the slightest annoyance. A *Courier-Journal* reporter recorded for posterity some of the sightseers' comments:

"There's the way they [the kidnappers] brought him [Gates] here!"

"There's the room where he was held prisoner!"

"There's where he killed him!"

"There's where he leaped off the porch!"

Investigation revealed that Richard Heaton had planned his revenge scheme for months and spent thousands of dollars on it, and this was in the days when you could buy a lot more with a buck. He had hired a female private detective from Chicago, Mrs. Jennie Moore, to keep an eye on his wife for several weeks. He had rented a house, purchased that surgical equipment and (as we shall see) hired a second detective to help accomplish his plot. Mary Heaton told detectives that she had been afraid her vengeance-crazed husband would also kill her and their two children. Detectives noted that the ropes binding William Gates had been cut and wondered how he got hold of a gun. They theorized that Mary helped him, which she denied.

Gates surrendered to the police on the morning of March 9. His story corroborated Mary Heaton's in all major details. During Gates's ordeal, Heaton's business partner, William A. Fisher, had dropped by the rented

house. Heaton told him confidentially: "I've got a man upstairs who has wronged me." At Heaton's request, Fisher stood guard over William, who was lying tied up on the mattress, while Heaton took a nap for half an hour. When he returned, he promised his partner that he only intended to give the guy upstairs a good scare and that if Fisher told anyone, he would kill him. Fisher took him at his word and didn't go to the police.

(Fisher would later admit under oath that he visited the house not once but twice. Yet he didn't dare breathe a word. Fisher had a healthy fear of his business partner.)

The police asked Gates how he escaped. He was armed with a pistol and a derringer when captured by his alleged best friend. Heaton confiscated the pistol but overlooked the smaller gun, which Gates used to save himself when the opportunity arose. He explained

Above: Mrs. Moore, the female detective. *Louisville Courier-Journal*, March 12, 1924. *Courtesy of the* Courier-Journal.

Opposite: Rear view of Heaton's house. The *X* marks the bedroom where the violence occurred. *Louisville Courier-Journal*, March 10, 1924. *Courtesy of the* Courier-Journal.

that Richard gave him an ineffective dose of chloroform. Pretending to be under the influence, William invented a clever story that bought him some time: he muttered that he had suspected Richard might murder him one of these days and sent a letter to a distant aunt along the lines of "If anything should happen to me, Richard Heaton is to blame." Richard mulled over this unexpected development, and the delay was fatal. After he freed William for a bathroom break, the captive shot him in the chest and neck. This explained the mysteries of how Gates was loosed from his bonds and where he got the gun he used for self-defense.

There was another question: who were the two men who helped Heaton abduct Gates? One had been located immediately, though it took a day for law enforcement to realize it. Heyde Conrad, an organist who played at the Rialto Theater, told detectives that he spent the night of March 8 at the house at the invitation of his old friend, the late Richard Heaton. Sure, he said, he heard someone in the house groaning as if in pain, but even though he "couldn't sleep for the noise," he didn't think it worth investigating. He also thought it odd that a stranger was staying in the house that night, acting like a guard. All Heyde knew about this fellow was that he was really tall and called himself "Frank." Later that night, at Richard's request, Heyde drove Frank to the station, where the giant boarded the ten thirty train and left town. Heyde breathlessly told the authorities that he believed "the big man was hired by Heaton to abduct Gates, carry him to the house and help torture him."

The room where Gates was held. *Louisville Courier-Journal*, March 9, 1924. *Courtesy of the* Courier-Journal.

Organist Heyde Conrad.
Louisville Courier-Journal,
March 9, 1924. *Courtesy of the*
Courier-Journal.

Detectives found the organist's claims of innocence and naivete impossible to believe. Before long, Heyde admitted that he was not just a bystander but one of the two men who helped Richard Heaton abduct the man he took to be a romantic rival. The other—the man called Frank—was easily found. He was an Indianapolis private detective, Frank Cordell, who protested that when Heaton hired him, he used the pseudonym "Peter Brooks" and that he, Cordell, knew nothing about the castration plot. All he knew was that he had been hired to help capture William Gates in Heaton's office and take him to the rented house. Heaton had explained to Cordell darkly: "Someone has stolen some stuff from me." Somehow Cordell didn't become suspicious that something sinister was afoot when Heaton snapped handcuffs on his friend's wrists. Cordell insisted he didn't know what Heaton intended to do with his prisoner and added, "I didn't ask."

On March 10, the grand jury indicted organist Conrad and detective Cordell for conspiring to imprison and commit mayhem against William Gates. On the same day, Gates, who had been arrested for murder, was released on bond. Mrs. Heaton talked to prosecutors on March 11. They refused to release details but hinted that what she said did not bode well for Conrad and Cordell.

According to the press, salesman Leslie Bishop said that a man resembling Richard Heaton had dropped by his establishment on February 14 and expressed an interest in purchasing his wares. Since Bishop sold caskets—and the potential customer did not give his name and asked Bishop questions about how caskets are buried in cemeteries—one might logically conclude that Heaton's original plan was to stuff his victim in a coffin and bury him on the sly. Bishop disappointed his would-be customer by stating that caskets weren't exactly novelty items and he could only sell to licensed undertakers.

On March 12, the public heard of someone previously unmentioned in the case: Dr. Edgar Clark, who claimed to have been on the scene when Heaton died in the rented house. On the night of the murder, he had received a phone call (he still didn't know from whom) requesting

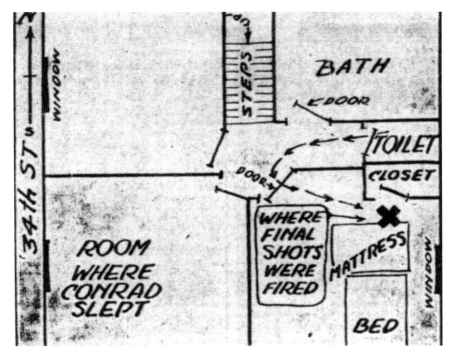

Diagram of the house's second floor. *Louisville Courier-Journal*, March 10, 1924. *Courtesy of the Courier-Journal.*

his presence at 637 South Thirty-Fourth Street—where, by a stupendous coincidence, Dr. Clark himself used to live. When he had arrived, he found Dr. Schoonover plying his trade.

When Mrs. Heaton was questioned before the coroner's jury, she described her husband as pathologically jealous and abusive:

> *Q. Was he of that jealous and suspicious character?*
> *A. Yes, sir.*
> *Q. Did he ever at any time before that falsely accuse you of infidelity with other men?*
> *A. Yes, sir.*
> *Q. Did he make exhaustive investigations about those matters?*
> *A. Yes, sir.*
> *Q. Did he travel around the country investigating?*
> *A. Yes, sir.*
> *Q. About how long did he consume in these investigations, how much time?*
> *A. About four years.*

Detectives inspecting Heaton's surgical gear. *Louisville Courier-Journal*, March 9, 1924. *Courtesy of the* Courier-Journal.

Q. About how much did he spend? What did he tell you?

A. *He said $75,000.* [Modern equivalent: $866,000. Heaton took revenge seriously.]

Q. Did he ever at any time find anything to justify his suspicions after returning from these trips?

A. *No, sir.*

She also revealed that he had attempted unsuccessfully to hypnotize her, for reasons unknown.

On March 14, the coroner's jury ruled that Gates's slaying of Heaton was justifiable. But he wasn't off the hook yet, as another twist in the already bizarre case was just around the corner.

It turned out this wasn't the first time Richard Heaton had pulled off such a scheme. Authorities in Lake City, South Carolina, said they recognized him as a man calling himself "Clem Rainey," who, along with a henchman, had in December 1923 abducted Mr. Wall, a former army lieutenant at Louisville's Camp Zachary Taylor. They used an unidentified woman as bait and held him prisoner in a swamp for hours. Heaton kidnapped him because he believed the ex-officer was having a fling with his wife but turned him loose after becoming convinced of his innocence. And his accomplice was—William Gates. Far from being a persecuted innocent, Gates had recently aided Heaton in the same sort of abduction plot that nearly resulted in his own gelding. It also suggests profound mental illness in the creepily obsessive Heaton, who organized an expedition to a distant state to track down and seize a man he merely suspected of committing adultery with Mrs. Heaton. The two strangers had fled back to Kentucky, but they were wanted in South Carolina for conspiracy, assault and battery and imprisonment.

In fact, Heaton and his future victim Gates made a habit out of abducting, handcuffing and abusing men. On March 15—only a day after Gates was acquitted in Louisville— W.W. Anderson, a garage owner of Houston, Texas, charged him with kidnapping and assault with intent to murder. Anderson said that on January 4, 1924, two men arrived in Houston, whom he now recognized as Gates and Heaton after seeing their pictures in the papers. Pretending to be sellers of oil leases, they inveigled Anderson to get in their car. Twelve miles from the city, one of them pulled a gun. They forced Anderson to walk into the forest, where they handcuffed him to a tree on the Crosby Road and beat him. Twenty-four hours later, they released him. And why did they do it? The reader will not be surprised to learn that Heaton was convinced Anderson had been sleeping with his wife.

Top: The long-suffering Mrs. Heaton. *Louisville Courier-Journal*, March 11, 1924. *Courtesy of the* Courier-Journal.

Bottom: The supremely jealous Mr. Heaton. *Louisville Courier-Journal*, March 11, 1924. *Courtesy of the* Courier-Journal.

The governor of South Carolina sent an extradition request to Kentucky's Governor Fields, who turned it down on the grounds that Gates's testimony was needed for the pending trials of Heaton's flunkies, Frank

Cordell and Heyde Conrad. Once their trials were completed, said Fields, South Carolina could have Gates and try him for the kidnapping of Mr. Wall.

Attorneys for Heaton's accomplices requested separate trials. Detective Cordell's began on April 8. William Gates reluctantly testified against the Indiana detective. To be more precise, Gates was reluctant to admit anything that might incriminate himself, such as the exact reason Heaton asked Gates to accompany him on a monthlong visit to Houston. The most he would say was that "he went there to locate a certain man and that he had found him." He also confessed to going on a road trip with Heaton to Lake City, South Carolina, to find out "whether or not another and different man was located there."

On the stand, Cordell said he was hired by Heaton to subdue and spirit away Gates but had been told only that Gates was an embezzler: "I thought…it was just an affair between employee and employer and figured that they wanted to talk it over for the purpose of settling it out of court, which is often done in cases where private detectives are called in." He denied that he had been in the room where Gates was held captive and had no idea anything about the situation was fishy until a *Courier-Journal* reporter called him after he returned to Indiana. On April 10, the jury found detective Cordell guilty of assault and sentenced him to sixty days in jail.

The trial for theater organist Heyde Conrad was scheduled for June 2, but it appears charges were dropped and nothing further was done with him. There is no record that he was tried.

And what became of the once-notorious "torture house" at 637 South Thirty-Fourth Street? After it achieved unwanted fame, the house was kept locked up tight and the neighbors were as wary of it as if it were haunted. On the night of Friday, June 13, 1924, passersby saw the basement light come on. Then other rooms were illuminated until "the whole house was lighted up." Spooked neighbors watched from across the street, afraid to investigate too closely. They could see no one inside. At midnight, the lights went out one by one, until the house was engulfed in darkness. When police investigated, they found that the culprits were not ghosts but mortal burglars who entered the back door using a skeleton key. The place had been thoroughly ransacked "from basement to attic." "The contents of every drawer and closet had been scattered about the floors," wrote a reporter. Even the mattress on which Gates had spent a mighty apprehensive three days was ripped open. What the intruders were

Left: Detective Cordell, the mysterious "Frank." *Louisville Courier-Journal*, March 12, 1924. *Courtesy of the* Courier-Journal.

Right: William Gates. Perhaps that's the hat he retrieved at great peril? It does seem a nice one. *Louisville Courier-Journal*, March 11, 1924. *Courtesy of the* Courier-Journal.

looking for no one could imagine, but police theorized Richard Heaton might have hidden money in the rented house—perhaps getaway cash, since he withdrew a large amount from his bank account a few days before his murder but only a few dollars were found on his body. One wonders why thieves would draw attention by turning on every light in the house they were burgling.

One person was most unhappy with the house's newly acquired sinister reputation: its owner, Mrs. Lula Hoke. On September 22, she filed suit in circuit court against the Louisville Trust Company, administrators of Heaton's estate, complaining that the murder caused the house's property value to depreciate a whole $3,000 (a bit less than $35,000 in modern currency). Mrs. Hoke wanted $4,648, which included $800 for lost rentals and $848 for damage Heaton did to the house. This somewhat less-than-ideal renter had torn out plumbing, removed light fixtures, damaged the plaster, tossed out his landlady's private papers and destroyed fruit trees in the yard. Oh yeah, and he got murdered there, making the place unsellable.

An old house stands now at that address that matches the architecture of adjacent dwellings, but a comparison with news photos from 1924 indicates that either it has been so heavily remodeled over the years as to be unrecognizable or the original "torture house" was razed long ago and a new home constructed on the site, which seems likely, given the physical (not to mention psychical) damage Heaton did to the place. Anyway, if it is the original house, and should the current owner hear ghostly sounds emanating from a second floor back bedroom, he or she might try addressing the revenant as "Richard." Let me know if anything happens.

BIBLIOGRAPHY

How McLaughlin Bit Off a Nose and Cheated the Hangman

Louisville Courier-Journal. "Bloody Memories." December 5, 1870, 3.
Louisville Journal. "The Fire, Which We Noticed Yesterday." April 20, 1842, 2.
———. "A Gentleman from Shelbyville." March 29, 1843, 3.
———. "Kentucky Legislature." January 13, 1844, 3.
———. "McLaughlin Convicted." March 31, 1843, 2.
———. "McLaughlin, the Murderer." May 6, 1843, 2.
———. "McLaughlin the Suicide." May 5, 1843, 2.
———. "Suicide of McLaughlin." April 29, 1843, 3.
———. "To the Editors." April 14, 1843, 2.
———. "We Learn from Shelby." April 1, 1843, 3.
———. "We Learn from Shelbyville." March 28, 1843, 3.
———. "We Learn from Shelbyville." March 30, 1843, 3.

Mind Over Matter

Louisville Journal. "A Man Named James Peters." August 24, 1852, 3.
———. "Baker, Who Was Shot." July 20, 1844, 3.
———. "James Peters, the Cripple." December 25, 1844, 3.
———. "Police Court." June 24, 1850, 3.
———. "Shooting." July 19, 1844, 3.

On the Dangers of Political Humor

Louisville Courier. "We See by the Memoranda." November 4, 1846, 3.
Louisville Courier-Journal. "Bloody Memories." December 5, 1870, 3.
Louisville Journal. "An Affair of Blood." September 28, 1842, 2.
———. "Closing Scene of a Locofoco Meeting." September 20, 1842, 2.
———. "Coroner's Inquest." October 7, 1842, 3.
———. "Death of Leonard Bliss, Jr." October 7, 1842, 3.
———. "Died." October 7, 1842, 3.
———. "Police Court." October 10, 1842, 3.
———. "Police Office." September 29, 1842, 2.
———. "Police Office." October 3, 1842, 2.
———. "The trial of Godfrey Pope…" April 17, 1843, 2.
———. "We Are Probably Expected to Give the Particulars." September 27, 1842, 3.
———. "We Are Requested to Say That the Many Calls." September 30, 1842, 3.

A Thing of Beauty Is a Joy Forever

Louisville Courier. "Police Court." January 27, 1853, 3.
Louisville Journal. "Arrest of Keats." September 27, 1850, 3.
———. "Criminal Court." October 18, 1850, 3.
———. "Escaped from Jail." September 26, 1850, 3.
———. "In the Criminal Court on Saturday." October 21, 1850, 2.
———. "Keats Pardoned." January 20, 1851, 3.
———. "Keats, Who Slew his Wife." December 18, 1850, 3.
———. "Marshal McMichael Returned." June 28, 1850, 3.
———. "Murder." June 25, 1850, 3.
———. "The Murderer Arrested." July 2, 1850, 3.
———. "Police Court." July 3, 1850, 3.

It Is All for Nothing

Louisville Courier. "Acquitted: Mr. Head." September 8, 1854, 3.
———. "Another Murder; A Place of Blood." March 31, 1860, 1.
———. "As We Had Expected, Mr. John H. Wheeler." June 8, 1853, 3.

———. "The Brutal and Unprovoked Murder." November 21, 1851, 3.

———. "Change of Venue." January 14, 1852, 3.

———. "Change of Venue." July 7, 1852, 3.

———. "Committed for Murder." November 25, 1851, 3.

———. "Conviction of Howard." November 22, 1852, 3.

———. "Criminal Term of the Oldham Circuit Court." November 20, 1852, 3.

———. "Dead!" November 20, 1851, 3.

———. "Excitement." February 4, 1853, 3

———. "Howard." June 30, 1853, 3.

———. "Howard Respited." January 12, 1853, 3.

———. "Howard, the Murderer." January 20, 1853, 3.

———. "Howard, the Murderer." February 1, 1853, 3.

———. "Howard, the Murderer." April 15, 1853, 3.

———. "Howard, the Murderer." April 18, 1853, 3.

———. "Howard, the Murderer." January 14, 1857, 3.

———. "Howard, the Murderer—His Escape." February 1, 1853, 3.

———. "Indictments at La Grange." February 12, 1853, 3.

———. "It Was Rumored in the City." February 2, 1853, 3.

———. "It Was Rumored on the Streets." February 8, 1853, 3.

———. "It Will Be Seen by Our Report of the Circuit Court." December 17, 1851, 3.

———. "La Grange Jailer and Guard Held to Bail." February 14, 1853, 3.

———. "Messrs. Editors." February 15, 1853, 2.

———. "Murderous Assault." November 19, 1851, 3.

———. "Petition for Pardon." January 27, 1853, 3.

———. "Police Court." November 25, 1851, 3.

———. "Probable Capture of Howard." June 29, 1853, 3.

———. "A Story of the Past." April 2, 1860, 1.

———. "There Was a Great Deal of Excitement." November 20, 1851, 3.

———. "The Trial of Head." September 7, 1854, 3.

———. "Trial of Howard—Fourth Day." November 19, 1852, 3.

———. "The Trial of William Howard." November 17, 1852, 3.

CAUTION: ELECTRICITY

Louisville Courier. "An Outrageous Assault." December 4, 1860, 1.

———. "Dave Caution, the Slave Convicted." January 21, 1861, 1.

———. "The Execution of the Slave Dave Caution." January 26, 1861, 1.

———. "The Last Hours of Dave Caution." January 25, 1861, 1.

———. "Wash Davis, the Sheriff." January 23, 1861, 1.

Louisville Courier-Journal. "Gone to Her Rest." July 17, 1871, 4.

A BUNCH OF BENJAMINS

Louisville Courier. "Another Deed of Blood." October 7, 1854, 3.

———. "Criminal Court." July 16, 1855, 4.

———. "Held to Bail." October 6, 1854, 3.

———. "Jury Hung." July 17, 1855, 4.

———. "Police Court." October 6, 1854, 3.

———. "Police Court." October 9, 1854, 3.

———. "Shooting Affair." October 3, 1854, 3.

———. "We Regret to Learn." October 5, 1854, 3.

———. "We Understand That in the Case of Ben Johnson." July 19, 1855, 4.

Louisville Courier-Journal. "Met His Father's Fate." March 3, 1888, 1.

HE'S A MANIAC, MANIAC ON THE FLOOR

Louisville Courier-Journal. "Boone County Correspondence." October 14, 1876, 2.

———. "Delighting the Demented." November 23, 1876, 1.

———. "Probably a Murder." October 5, 1876, 1.

———. "The Regular Monthly Dance." November 22, 1876, 4.

———. "William Henry Harrison." October 5, 1876, 3.

AND A MERRY CHRISTMAS TO YOU, TOO!

Louisville Courier-Journal. "Before Heaven's Bar." March 25, 1890, 2.

Louisville Journal. "A Midnight Murder." December 24, 1866, 2.

———. "Continuance of the Mendel Murder Case." February 8, 1867, 2.

———. "Jefferson Circuit Court." May 23, 1867, 2.

———. "The Mendel Case." January 14, 1867, 2.

———. "The Mendel Murder." January 12, 1867, 2.

———. "The Mendel Murder Case." February 7, 1867, 3.

———. "The Mendel Parricide." May 20, 1867, 2.

———. "The Mendel Trial." May 21, 1867, 2.

———. "The Next Case Before the Court." January 7, 1867, 2.

———. "Postponed." January 2, 1867, 2.

First, Do No Harm

Louisville Courier-Journal. "Bond Forfeited." February 8, 1870, 4.

———. "Dr. Collins Acquitted." July 4, 1868, 4.

———. "Dr. Collins Again." January 31, 1870, 4.

———. "Dr. George F. Collins." April 15, 1868, 2.

———. "Hon. Judge Stites." May 3, 1868, 2.

———. "Louisville City Court." February 15, 1868, 2.

———. "The Manly Tragedy." February 14, 1868, 2.

———. "The Mt. Washington Tragedy." February 1, 1870, 4.

———. "Murder on the Highway." February 13, 1868, 2.

Sabetti, Mary L., and Doris Owen. *Bullitt County Cemeteries, Vol. 2.* N.p., 1989.

Josephine Lawrence Misses the Target

Louisville Courier-Journal. "Another Tragedy." May 19, 1870, 4.

———. "The Bar Room Tragedy." May 20, 1870, 4.

———. "A Blood-Stained Record." November 20, 1870, 4.

———. "The Case of Josephine Lawrence." May 21, 1870, 4.

———. "A Champion Assaultist." September 17, 1872, 4.

———. "Disorderly Conduct." May 11, 1884, 11.

———. "Disorderly Conduct." April 21, 1888, 6.

———. "Disorderly Conduct." April 28, 1888, 8.

———. "Disorderly Conduct." January 11, 1889, 8.

———. "Disorderly Conduct." December 30, 1897, 8.

———. "The Examining Trial." June 6, 1870, 4.

———. "Fight About Lambs." May 10, 1896, 7.

———. "Hand of the Humane Society." January 23, 1896, 8.

———. "In the Ordinance Court." June 5, 1891, 2.

———. "Jefferson Circuit Court." January 3, 1872, 3.

———. "Jefferson Circuit Court." May 7, 1872, 4.

———. "Jefferson Circuit Court." May 9, 1872, 3.

———. "Josephine Lawrence, the Lewd Woman." July 12, 1870, 4.

———. "Josephine Lawrence, the Woman Who Shot." August 16, 1870, 4.

———. "Josephine Lawrence Waived." May 24, 1870, 4.

———. "Josephine Lawrence Was Brought." June 7, 1870, 4.

———. "Mike Lang, the Man from Peru." May 23, 1870, 4.

———. "Moved Stable and All." January 23, 1886, 8.

———. "Murder." June 4, 1870, 4.

———. "One Indictment." March 18, 1900, 13.

———. "Proceedings in Court Yesterday." May 14, 1890, 6.

———. "Terry Ridge Swindled Firemen." October 11, 1894, 6.

Mr. Miller Goes to Gambling Hell

Louisville Courier-Journal. "Col. Phil Lee's Argument." July 15, 1869, 4.

———. "The Croxton Case." July 3, 1869, 4.

———. "The Croxton Trial." July 7, 1869, 4.

———. "The Croxton Trial." July 8, 1869, 4.

———. "The Fifth Street Homicide." July 10, 1869, 1.

———. "The Fifth Street Tragedy." April 25, 1869, 4.

———. "The Gambling House Tragedy." April 29, 1869, 4.

———. "The Gamblers." March 14, 1885, 6.

———. "Jefferson Circuit Court." July 7, 1869, 4.

———. "No Jury." July 4, 1869, 4.

———. "Not Guilty." July 11, 1869, 4.

———. "A Pamphlet History." October 3, 1869, 4.

———. "Shocking Tragedy." April 24, 1869, 4.

———. "Trial of Joseph Croxton." July 2, 1869, 4.

Louisville Journal. "Murder." December 22, 1845, 3.

———. "Some of Our Readers." December 29, 1845, 2.

———. "We Are Informed." December 25, 1845, 2.

"And Wife"

Louisville Courier-Journal. "Both Letters Were Written by Nellie McCubbin." September 17, 1898, 10.

———. "Guilty Love Causes Death of Three People." September 16, 1898, 8.

———. "Third Note." September 18, 1898, I, 7.

———. "The Wages of Sin." September 16, 1898, 4.

WORKPLACE VIOLENCE

Louisville Courier-Journal. "Badly Whipped." June 25, 1872, 4.

———. "The Bloody Knife." May 30, 1872, 4.

———. "A Death Wound." June 20, 1872, 4.

———. "An Illegal Inquest." June 23, 1872, 4.

———. "The Intended Second Inquest." June 25, 1872, 4.

———. "The Stabbing on the *Burns*." May 31, 1872, 4.

VALENTINE IS DONE

Louisville Courier-Journal. "Condemned to Death." December 22, 1871, 4.

———. "The County Murder." June 29, 1871, 4.

———. "Doomed." September 26, 1872, 4.

———. "Doomed for Murder." June 30, 1872, 4.

———. "Found Guilty of Murder." December 7, 1871, 4.

———. "The Gallows." December 22, 1871, 3.

———. "The Gallows." May 25, 1872, 4.

———. "Gone to Another Judge." October 27, 1874, 4.

———. "The Price of a Sweetheart." June 27, 1871, 4.

———. "Small Talk." May 30, 1872, 3.

———. "Was He Guilty?" November 22, 1874, 3.

COFFEE, EXTRA BITTER

Louisville Courier. "The Fatal Poisoning Case." July 31, 1857, 3.

———. "Jefferson Circuit Court." January 21, 1858, 2.

———. "Jefferson Circuit Court." May 11, 1858, 1.

———. "John A. Comstock." January 21, 1858, 2.

———. "Marriage Licenses." November 26, 1859, 1.

———. "Poisoned." July 29, 1857, 3.

———. "The Poisoning Case." July 30, 1857, 3.

———. "The Poisoning Case." August 1, 1857, 3.

———. "The Poisoning Case." August 5, 1857, 1.

———. "The Poisoning Case." August 5, 1857, 3.

———. "The Poisoning Case." October 15, 1857, 3.

———. "The Poisoning Case." October 16, 1857, 3.

———. "Police Court." July 29, 1857, 1.

———. "Police Court." August 1, 1857, 1.

———. "Police Court." August 3, 1857, 1.

How Tom Smith Brought Unwarranted Disrepute upon the Croton Oil Industry

Louisville Courier. "A Case Worse Than Heathen Cruelty." June 8, 1857, 2.

———. "Horrible Effects of the Smallpox." February 11, 1846, 3.

———. "Smallpox." October 1, 1846, 3.

———. "The Smallpox Is Said." January 21, 1846, 2.

———. "A Smallpox Panic." April 13, 1861, 1.

———. "The Way John Jackson Got Off." January 19, 1858, 1.

Louisville Courier-Journal. "Among the Slayers." March 19, 1873, 4.

———. "The Breeden Murder." May 24, 1871, daily edition, 4.

———. "*Brownsville States*." May 21, 1873, 2.

———. "Cadiz, Ohio." September 13, 1871, 2.

———. "The Croton Oil Business." March 30, 1873, 1.

———. "The Croton Oil Case." May 11, 1873, 4.

———. "The Croton Oil Case." May 21, 1873, 4.

———. "The Croton Oil Case." May 23, 1873, 4.

———. "The Croton Oil Case." May 25, 1873, 3.

———. "A Curious Funeral Ceremony." May 12, 1873, 4.

———. "The Doom of the Murderers." November 29, 1872, 4.

———. "Doomed to Death." March 27, 1873, 3.

———. "The Execution Last Friday." March 30, 1873, 4.

———. "Expiation." March 29, 1873, 1.

———. "The Fugitive Murderer." December 2, 1872, 4.

———. "Gone to His Death." November 30, 1872, 4.

———. "*Hawesville Plaindealer*." March 3, 1874, 2.

———. "Jefferson County Court." May 21, 1873, 3.

———. "The Law's Last Penalty." March 29, 1873, 4.

———. "The McKenzie." January 30, 1873, 2.

———. "The Murder in the County." May 20, 1871, 4.

———. "Reading the Death Warrant." January 22, 1873, 4.

———. "The Recaptured Murderer." December 5, 1872, 1.

———. "The Result of the Investigation." May 21, 1873, 1.

———. "Says the Bolivar." April 1, 1872, 2.

———. "Scared to Death." April 5, 1872, 1.

———. "A Sharp Dodge." December 4, 1872, 4.

———. "A Sick Woman Left to Die." June 25, 1872, 3.

———. "Tom Smith." March 28, 1873, 4.

———. "A Verdict Was Rendered." May 21, 1873, 4.

———. "Waxahachie." February 3, 1873, 2.

———. "We Publish This Morning a Short but Manly Letter." March 30, 1873, 2.

———. "Whose Fault Is It?" December 13, 1872, 4.

———. "Yesterday's Execution." March 29, 1873, 2.

Louisville Journal. "A Negro Woman Died." March 16, 1866, 1.

———. "Rome, Perry County." February 2, 1864, 1.

———. "Smallpox." December 8, 1864, 3.

EVERYTHING LOOKS LOVELIER BY CANDLELIGHT

Louisville Courier-Journal. "The Case of Jacob Doup." October 21, 1873, 4.

———. "Daub, the Wife Murderer." November 7, 1873, 4.

———. "Death of Jacob Daub." December 6, 1874, 4.

———. "Dying Condition of a Murderer." December 5, 1874, 4.

———. "Horrible Murder." October 17, 1873, 4.

———. "Jacob Daub, the Wife Murderer." October 22, 1873, 4.

———. "Jacob Doup." October 18, 1873, 4.

———. "The Murderers." January 30, 1874, 4.

MURDERS-IN-LAW

Mrs. Klanner

Louisville Courier-Journal. "Condition of Mrs. Klanner." December 26, 1871, 4.

———. "Death of Mrs. Klanner." December 27, 1871, daily edition, 4.

———. "Jefferson Circuit Court." January 14, 1872, 4.

———. "The Mother-In-Law Murder." December 29, 1871, 4.

———. "Murderous Attack." December 25, 1871, 4.

———. "The Terrible Tragedy Which Occurred." December 30, 1871, 2.
———. "The Weisert Murder." December 28, 1871, 4.
———. "Mrs. Weisert, Who Killed." January 3, 1872, daily edition, 4.

Tom Cooke

Louisville Courier-Journal. "The Cook Case Again." January 20, 1874, 4.
———. "Devoured in Flames." August 22, 1873, 4.
———."A Horrible Tragedy." January 3, 1874, 4.
———. "Jealousy and Gore." January 1, 1874, 4.
———. "A Murderer's Wife." November 27, 1875, 4.
———. "New Albany." January 7, 1874, 4.
———. "The Recent Tragedy." January 6, 1874, 4.
———. "Tom Cook Assaults His Keeper." May 19, 1876, 1.
———. "Tom Cook Was Indicted." January 21, 1874, 4.
———. "Tom Cooke." October 2, 1874, 4.
———. "The Trial of Tom Cook." September 28, 1874, 4.
———. "The Twin Tragedies." January 4, 1874, 4.
———. "Yesterday's Tragedy." January 3, 1874, 1.

Sweeney and Fenn Beg to Differ

Louisville Courier. "The Blood List." January 4, 1858, 2.
———. "Inquest No. 18." April 2, 1857, 3.
———. "Jefferson Criminal Court." October 16, 1858, 1.
———. "Jefferson Criminal Court." October 18, 1858, 2.
———. "The Late Murder." April 2, 1857, 3.
———. "A Murderer Pardoned." August 31, 1859, 1.
———. "The Murder of Casper Fenn." April 6, 1857, 1.
———. "Murder Trial." October 16, 1857, 3.
———. "Two Murderers Committed." April 6, 1857, 3

The Morgue, the Merrier, or Grave Errors

Louisville Courier-Journal. "All a Mistake." December 16, 1876, 4.
———. "The Body of Martin Monahan." December 19, 1876, 4.
———. "Clearing Up." December 15, 1876, 1.

———. "Free as a Bird." December 19, 1876, 4.

———. "Identified." December 18, 1876, 4.

———. "Martin Monahan." December 26, 1876, 4.

———. "Most Mysterious." December 13, 1876, 4.

———. "The Murdered Man Buried." January 5, 1877, 4.

———. "Random Speculations." December 30, 1876, 4.

———. "Rather Astounding!" December 25, 1876, 4.

———. "Resurrected." December 28, 1876, 4.

———. "The Unknown Murdered Man." December 17, 1876, 1.

———. "Viewing the Corpse." December 29, 1876, 4.

———. "Wet Woods Murder Again." January 4, 1877, 4.

A FORMER SLAVE FINDS FRIENDS

Louisville Courier-Journal. "Actually Cremated." December 9, 1877, 1.

———. "Booked for Death." October 3, 1878, 4.

———. "The Condemned Croomes." October 1, 1878, 4.

———. "The Cremated Woman." December 10, 1877, 4.

———. "Crooms' Criminality." December 13, 1877, 4.

———. "Doomed to Die." September 19, 1878, 4.

———. "End of His Rope." September 13, 1878, 3.

———. "Execution Postponed by the Governor." October 4, 1878, 4.

———. "Henry Crooms Was Indicted." December 15, 1877, 6.

———. "In Defense of Crooms." September 20, 1878, 4.

———. "Not to Hang Today." October 4, 1878, 4.

———. "On Behalf of Crooms." October 2, 1878, 4.

———. "Saved from the Scaffold." November 6, 1878, 2.

———. "To Be Hanged." February 9, 1878, 1.

WHEN JURISDICTIONS COLLIDE

Louisville Courier-Journal. "Awaiting Death." April 28, 1869, 4.

———. "Capital Punishment." April 20, 1869, 4.

———. "The Conley Case." May 15, 1869, 3.

———. "The Conley-Polk Murder." December 2, 1868, 4.

———. "Execution." April 10, 1869, 4.

———. "Execution of Conley." May 18, 1869, 4.

————. "The Gallows." March 15, 1872, 4.

————. "A Government Negro." May 20, 1869, 4.

————. "John Conley." May 1, 1869, 4.

————. "Murder in the Woods." June 1, 1868, 4.

————. "The Negro Murderer." December 6, 1868, 4.

————. "The Negro Murderer." January 12, 1869, 4.

————. "The Negro Tragedy." June 2, 1868, 4.

————. "New Trials." February 5, 1869, 4.

————. "Petition for the Reprieve of Conley." April 28, 1869, 4.

————. "The Pet of the Courts." June 5, 1869, 4.

————. "Prison and Gallows." February 28, 1869, 4.

————. "The Reprieved." April 18, 1872, 4.

————. "Shanahan and Conley Not to Be Hung." April 17, 1872, 4.

————. "A Slander on Kentucky." May 6, 1869, 2.

————. "Small Talk." April 18, 1872, 3.

————. "Still Mixed." May 23, 1869, 4.

————. "To Hang or Not to Hang." April 30, 1869, 4.

ATTEMPTED GLAND THEFT

Louisville Courier-Journal. "Another Doctor at Heaton's Death." March 13, 1924, 1+.

————. "Confesses His Part in Abduction." March 10, 1924, 1+.

————. "Conrad, Cordell to Face Trial Today." April 8, 1924, 1.

————. "Cordell Details Gates Kidnapping." April 10, 1924, 1+.

————. "Cordell Given 60 Days in Jail." April 11, 1924, 1.

————. "Extradition Hearing for Gates Today." March 22, 1924, 1.

————. "Fields Denies Requisitions in Heaton Case." March 23, 1924, 1.

————. "Fisher Tells of Visiting House." March 11, 1924, 3.

————. "Gates Bares Torture Plot Details." March 10, 1924, 1+.

————. "Gates Bares Trips South with Heaton." April 8, 1924, 1.

————. "Gates' Slaying of Heaton Held Justifiable by Coroner's Jury." March 15, 1924, 1+.

————. "Gates Wanted in Two Kidnapping Cases." March 16, 1924, 1+.

————. "Heaton Torture House Owner Asks $4,648." September 23, 1924, 1+.

————. "Heaton Wills to Widow $250 Month for Life." March 18, 1924, 1+.

————. "Hidden Pistol Saved Victim." March 10, 1924, 1+.

————. "House of Heaton Plot Ransacked." June 15, 1924, I, 1+.

———. "Klan Link in Heaton Case Seen." March 17, 1924, 1+.

———. "Man Chained in Home 3 Days Kills Captor." March 9, 1924, I, 1+.

———. "Money Sought in 'Torture House.'" June 16, 1924, 1.

———. "Most Unusual Case in Years, Officials Say." March 10, 1924, 1.

———. "Mrs. Heaton Tells 'Several Important Facts' in Plot." March 12, 1924, 1+.

———. "Mrs. Heaton to Tell Her Story Today." March 14, 1924, 1+.

———. "Scene of Tragedy Is Surrounded by Curious Crowds." March 10, 1924, 1+.

———. "Slaying Foils Plot to Mutilate." March 9, 1924, I, 1+.

———. "Will Renounced by Mrs. Heaton." April 25, 1924, 10.

———. "Woman Detective in Heaton Case Tells Her Part in Plot." March 11, 1924, 3.

ABOUT THE AUTHOR

K even McQueen was born in Richmond, Kentucky, in 1967. He has degrees in English from Berea College and Eastern Kentucky University (EKU) and is a senior lecturer in composition and world literature at EKU. He has written twenty-three books on history, the supernatural, historical true crime, biography and many strange topics, covering nearly every region of the United States. In addition, he has made many appearances on radio, podcasts and television. Look him up on Facebook or at kevenmcqueenstories.com.